SARA L. WESTON

Ancient Female Shamans

This book was professionally typeset on Reedsy.
Find out more at reedsy.com

Contents

Preface

In the captivating exploration that follows, "Ancient Female Shamans," we embark on a journey through the corridors of time to unveil the enigmatic realm of female shamans. Traditionally, the image of a shaman has been synonymous with masculinity, but the pages of history, when carefully examined, unfold a different narrative—one where the profound influence and mystical wisdom of female practitioners become apparent.

This book is a testament to the evolving understanding of shamanism, challenging preconceived notions and shedding light on the often-overlooked contributions of women in this ancient practice. As we delve into the troves of archaeological discoveries and embrace the insights brought forth by scientific progress, a rich tapestry emerges—one that showcases the pivotal role played by female shamans across diverse cultures and civilizations.

Prepare to be immersed in the stories of these extraordinary women who, despite the historical shadows that obscured their presence, wielded spiritual power, healing abilities, and visionary insights. Through research and a nuanced perspective, "Ancient Female Shamans" strives to rectify the imbalance in our comprehension of shamanic traditions and encourages a more inclusive appreciation of the sacred art of journeying between worlds.

1

Chapter 1

Overview

The book "Ancient Female Shamans" delves into the fascinating world of female shamans throughout history. While shamanism is often associated with males, recent archaeological and scientific advancements have revealed that shamans were both male and female. In Chapter 1, "Introduction to Ancient Female Shamans," readers are introduced to the historical overview of shamans, the origins of the word "shaman," and the roles and responsibilities of shamans in society. The chapter also challenges gender stereotypes by exploring the significant presence of female shamans in history.

Chapter 2, "Unveiling the Mythical Volva: Norse Female Shamans," focuses on the Norse mythology and the existence of the Volva. Through archaeological evidence, readers discover the reality of female shamans in Norse culture. The chapter explores the role of the Volva in Norse society and sheds light on the forgotten female shamans of Norse mythology.

In Chapter 3, "The Bad Dürrenberg Shaman Burial: A Glimpse into Ancient Practices," readers are taken on a journey to the discovery of the Bad Dürrenberg burial, a 9,000-year-old shaman burial. This chapter unravels the secrets of the burial, including the rituals and artifacts found, and interprets the significance of this ancient shaman's resting place. The legacy of the Bad Dürrenberg shaman is explored, shedding light on the practices and beliefs of ancient female shamans.

Chapter 4, "Women as Shamans: Leadership Roles in Ancient Civilizations," highlights the important role of women in shamanic practices and their leadership roles in ancient civilizations. Prominent female shamans in various ancient societies are discussed, emphasizing the power and influence they held. This chapter explores the enduring legacy of women in shamanic leadership, showcasing their contributions to their communities and societies.

The book "Ancient Female Shamans" uncovers the rituals, practices, symbolism, and tools of female shamans in Chapter 5 and 6. Readers gain insights into the healing and medicinal roles of shamans, their divination and prophecy practices, and their spiritual journeys through trance and ecstasy. The significance of ceremonies and rituals in connecting with the divine is also explored. Additionally, the symbolism and tools used by female shamans, such as animal spirits, sacred plants, drums, masks, and ritual artifacts, are examined in detail.

Chapter 7 delves into the spiritual and mystical beliefs of ancient female shamans. The cosmology and shamanic worldview are discussed, along with the connection between humans and the spirit world. The role of ancestors and ancestral spirits in shamanic practices is explored, as well as the shaman's journey into other realms.

In Chapter 8, the decline and suppression of female shamanism are examined. The rise of patriarchal societies and the marginalization of women in religious and cultural shifts are discussed. However, the legacy of female shamanism in modern times is also explored, along with efforts to revive and honor ancient female shamanic traditions.

Chapter 9 focuses on contemporary female shamans and their practices and beliefs. The challenges and opportunities faced by modern-day female shamans are discussed, highlighting their roles as healers and spiritual guides. The global impact of contemporary female shamanism is also examined, showcasing the relevance and influence of this ancient tradition in the modern world.

Finally, in Chapter 10, the book concludes by celebrating the legacy of ancient female shamans. The importance of recognizing and honoring female shamanism is emphasized, along with the lessons that can be learned from these remarkable women for modern society. The enduring influence of female shamans throughout history is explored, and the book encourages readers to embrace the wisdom and power of the feminine in shamanic practices.

Introduction to Ancient Female Shamans

1.1 Shamans: A Historical Overview

Shamans, often associated with male figures, have long been recognized as spiritual leaders and healers in various cultures around the world. However, archaeological and scientific advancements have revealed that shamans were not exclusively male but also included powerful and revered female practitioners. This chapter explores the historical significance of ancient female shamans and their contributions to society.

1.1.1 The Origins of the Word 'Shaman'

The term "shaman" originates from the Tungus people of Siberia, who used it to describe their spiritual leaders. The word itself has no gender-specific connotations, and it was only later that it became associated predominantly with male practitioners. The Tungus shamans were believed to have the ability to communicate with the spirit world, heal the sick, and provide guidance to their communities.

1.1.2 Shamans in Society: Roles and Responsibilities

Shamans held a unique and revered position within their societies. They were seen as intermediaries between the human and spirit realms, possessing the ability to connect with the divine and access hidden knowledge. Shamans were sought after for their healing abilities, as they were believed to have the power to cure illnesses and restore balance to individuals and communities.

Beyond their role as healers, shamans also served as spiritual guides, diviners, and mediators. They conducted rituals and ceremonies to communicate with spirits, interpret omens, and provide guidance for important decisions. In many cultures, shamans were considered the guardians of cultural traditions and the keepers of ancestral wisdom.

1.1.3 The Discovery of the Mythical Volva: Norse Female Shamans

One fascinating example of ancient female shamans is found in Norse mythology. The Volva, often depicted as wise women with prophetic abilities, played a significant role in Norse society. While some dismissed the Volva as mythical figures, archaeological evidence has shed light on their existence and importance.

Excavations at burial sites in Scandinavia have revealed artifacts and remains associated with female shamans. These findings provide tangible evidence of the Volva's existence and their integral role in Norse culture. The Volva were believed to possess the power of prophecy, divination, and healing, making them highly respected and sought-after figures in their communities.

1.1.4 The Bad Dürrenberg Shaman Burial: A Glimpse into Ancient Practices

Another remarkable discovery that highlights the presence of ancient female shamans is the 9,000-year-old shaman burial in Bad Dürrenberg, Germany. This burial site, dating back to the Mesolithic period, provides valuable insights into the rituals and practices of ancient shamans.

The Bad Dürrenberg burial contained the remains of a woman adorned with elaborate ceremonial objects, including a headdress made of red deer antlers and various animal bones. The presence of these artifacts suggests that the woman held a significant spiritual role within her community. The burial site also contained evidence of ritualistic practices, such as the inclusion of medicinal plants and the arrangement of the body in a fetal position.

This discovery challenges the prevailing notion that ancient shamans were exclusively male. It highlights the important role that women played in ancient societies as spiritual leaders and healers. The Bad Dürrenberg shaman burial serves as a testament to the rich and diverse history of female shamans and their contributions to ancient civilizations.

1.1.5 Women as Shamans: Leadership Roles in Ancient Civilizations

Throughout history, women have held prominent positions as shamans and spiritual leaders in various ancient civilizations. From the priestesses of ancient Egypt to the oracles of ancient Greece, female shamans played crucial roles in religious and societal affairs.

These women were not only healers but also leaders and decision-makers. They held positions of power and influence, guiding their communities through times of crisis and change. Female shamans were often revered for their wisdom, intuition, and ability to connect with the spiritual realm.

The presence of women in leadership roles within shamanic practices challenges the notion that ancient societies were solely patriarchal. It highlights the importance of recognizing the significant contributions of women in shaping the spiritual and cultural landscape of ancient civilizations.

The discoveries of ancient female shamans and their leadership roles provide valuable insights into the diverse and complex nature of ancient societies. They challenge gender stereotypes and shed light on the enduring legacy of women in shamanic practices. By acknowledging and honoring the contributions of these remarkable women, we can gain a deeper understanding of our shared human history and the power of the feminine in spiritual traditions.

1.2 The Origins of the Word 'Shaman'

The term 'shaman' is commonly associated with male spiritual leaders and healers in various cultures around the world. However, archaeological and anthropological research has revealed that shamans were not exclusively male but also included females who played significant roles in ancient societies. The word 'shaman' itself has an intriguing origin and carries a rich history that sheds light on the diverse practices and beliefs of ancient female shamans.

The term 'shaman' originates from the Tungusic language spoken by the indigenous peoples of Siberia. It was first introduced to the Western world by Russian explorers and scholars in the 17th century. The word 'shaman' refers to a person who possesses the ability to communicate with the spirit world and acts as an intermediary between the human and spiritual realms. The Tungusic word 'šamán' is believed to have derived from the Evenki language, meaning "one who knows" or "healer."

Shamans held a revered position in their societies, serving as healers, spiritual guides, and mediators between the physical and spiritual realms. They were believed to possess supernatural powers and the ability to communicate with spirits, ancestors, and deities. The role of a shaman varied across cultures, but their primary responsibilities included healing the sick, divination, performing rituals, and providing spiritual guidance to their communities.

The discovery of the mythical Volva from Norse mythology provides compelling evidence of the existence of female shamans in ancient cultures. In Norse mythology, the Volva was a powerful female seeress who possessed prophetic abilities and had a deep connection with the gods. While initially dismissed as mere mythological figures, archaeological findings have confirmed the presence of female shamans in Norse society.

Archaeological excavations have unearthed artifacts and burial sites that provide insights into the roles and practices of female shamans. One notable discovery is the 9,000-year-old shaman burial in Bad Dürrenberg, Germany. This burial site contained the remains of a woman adorned with ritual objects and surrounded by offerings. The presence of these artifacts suggests that she held a significant spiritual role within her community.

The discovery of ancient female shamans challenges the traditional narrative that portrays shamanism as a predominantly male domain. It highlights the important roles that women played in ancient civilizations, not only as healers but also as leaders and decision-makers. In many ancient societies, female shamans held positions of power and influence, guiding their communities in matters of spirituality, healing, and governance.

Prominent female shamans in ancient civilizations such as the Sumerians, Egyptians, and Celts demonstrate the widespread recognition and respect given to women in shamanic leadership roles. These women were revered for their wisdom, healing abilities, and their connection to the divine. They served as spiritual advisors, arbiters of justice, and custodians of sacred knowledge.

The discoveries of women as shamans provide valuable insights into the historical and cultural contexts in which they operated. They challenge the notion that women were solely confined to domestic roles and highlight the significant contributions they made to their societies. The power and influence of female shamans extended beyond their healing abilities, as they played pivotal roles in shaping the spiritual and social fabric of ancient civilizations.

The recognition of female shamans in ancient history is not only important for understanding the past but also for acknowledging the enduring legacy of women in shamanic practices. It serves as a reminder that women have always held positions of power and authority, even in societies where patriarchal structures dominated. By honoring and reviving the ancient traditions of female shamans, we can reclaim and celebrate the wisdom and power of the feminine in shamanic practices today.

1.3 Shamans in Society

Shamans, often associated with male figures, have long been recognized as spiritual leaders and healers in various cultures throughout history. However, archaeological and scientific advancements have shed light on the fact that shamans were not exclusively male but also included females who played significant roles in ancient societies. In this section, we will explore the diverse roles and responsibilities of shamans in society, the origins of the word "shaman," and the important discoveries of female shamans in ancient civilizations.

1.3.1 The Meaning and Origins of Shamanism

Before delving into the roles and responsibilities of shamans, it is essential to understand the meaning and origins of shamanism. The term "shaman" originated from the Tungus people of Siberia and refers to a spiritual practitioner who acts as an intermediary between the human and spirit worlds. Shamans are believed to possess the ability to communicate with spirits, perform healing rituals, and guide individuals through spiritual journeys.

1.3.2 Shamans in Ancient Societies

Shamans held a revered position in ancient societies, playing multifaceted roles that extended beyond their spiritual practices. They were often seen as healers, diviners, and advisors, providing guidance and support to their communities. Shamans possessed extensive knowledge of medicinal plants, rituals, and ceremonies, making them indispensable members of their societies.

In many cultures, shamans were responsible for maintaining the spiritual well-being of their communities. They performed rituals to ensure bountiful harvests, protect against evil spirits, and promote overall harmony. Shamans were also sought after for their abilities to communicate with the spirit world and provide insights into the future, making them valuable sources of guidance and prophecy.

1.3.3 Rediscovering Female Shamans: The Mythical Volva

One remarkable discovery that challenges the traditional perception of shamans as predominantly male figures is the existence of female shamans in Norse mythology. The Norse Volva, often depicted as wise women with prophetic abilities, played a crucial role in ancient Norse society. They were believed to possess the power to communicate with the gods, foretell the future, and provide spiritual guidance.

Archaeological evidence, such as the Oseberg ship burial in Norway, has revealed the presence of female shamans in Norse culture. The burial site contained artifacts associated with shamanic practices, including staffs, drums, and ritual objects. These findings provide tangible proof of the significant role that female shamans played in Norse society, challenging the notion that shamanism was exclusively a male domain.

1.3.4 Unveiling Ancient Shaman Burials: The Bad Dürrenberg Discovery

Another remarkable discovery that highlights the existence of female shamans is the 9,000-year-old shaman burial in Bad Dürrenberg, Germany. This burial site, dating back to the Mesolithic period, provides valuable insights into the practices and rituals of ancient female shamans.

The Bad Dürrenberg burial contained the remains of a woman adorned with elaborate jewelry and surrounded by various artifacts, including a headdress made of red deer antlers and a variety of animal bones. These artifacts suggest that the woman held a significant spiritual role within her community, possibly as a shaman. The discovery of this burial site reinforces the idea that female shamans were not only present but also held esteemed positions in ancient societies.

1.3.5 Female Shamans as Leaders in Ancient Civilizations

The discoveries of female shamans in various ancient civilizations have challenged the notion that women were solely relegated to subordinate roles. In cultures such as ancient Egypt, Mesopotamia, and the Indus Valley, women held positions of power and influence as shamans and spiritual leaders.

Female shamans in ancient civilizations often served as healers, diviners, and decision-makers. They played crucial roles in guiding their communities through times of crisis, providing spiritual guidance, and making important decisions. These women were respected and revered for their wisdom, knowledge, and ability to connect with the spiritual realm.

The existence of female shamans in leadership roles highlights the importance of recognizing the contributions of women in ancient societies. It challenges the patriarchal narratives that have often marginalized and suppressed the voices and roles of women throughout history.

In conclusion, the discovery of ancient female shamans has shattered the misconception that shamans were exclusively male figures. Archaeological and scientific advancements have provided evidence of the significant roles that women played as spiritual leaders, healers, and decision-makers in ancient societies. The existence of female shamans, such as the Volva in Norse mythology and the discoveries at the Bad Dürrenberg burial site, highlights the importance of recognizing and honoring the contributions of women in shamanic practices. These discoveries not only reshape our understanding of ancient civilizations but also inspire us to embrace the wisdom and power of the feminine in contemporary shamanic practices.

1.4 Challenging Gender Stereotypes

Throughout history, the image of a shaman has often been associated with males, but archaeological and scientific advances have challenged this gender stereotype. It is now widely accepted that shamans were both male and female, playing vital roles in ancient societies. In this section, we will explore the fascinating discoveries that have shed light on the existence and significance of female shamans in history.

1.4.1 The Shaman: Breaking Gender Barriers

To understand the significance of female shamans, it is essential to first grasp the concept of a shaman. The term "shaman" originated from the Tungus people of Siberia and refers to a spiritual practitioner who acts as an intermediary between the human and spirit worlds. Shamans are known for their ability to communicate with spirits, perform healing rituals, and guide their communities through various challenges.

1.4.2 The Origins of the Word 'Shaman'

The word "shaman" has its roots in the Tungus language, specifically the Evenki dialect. It entered the English language through Russian anthropologists who studied the indigenous peoples of Siberia. The term gained popularity in the late 19th century and has since become a widely recognized term to describe spiritual practitioners worldwide.

1.4.3 Shamans in Society: Roles and Responsibilities

Shamans held esteemed positions within their communities, serving as healers, diviners, and spiritual guides. They played crucial roles in maintaining the well-being and harmony of their societies. Shamans were responsible for healing the sick, providing spiritual guidance, and performing rituals to ensure the prosperity of their communities. Their knowledge of the spirit world and their ability to communicate with spirits made them indispensable figures in ancient societies.

1.4.4 Rediscovering the Forgotten Female Shamans

One of the most intriguing discoveries that challenge the notion of male-dominated shamanism is the existence of female shamans in Norse mythology. In Norse culture, female shamans were known as "volvas." These mythical figures were revered for their prophetic abilities and their connection to the gods. While some dismissed the volvas as mere mythological characters, archaeological evidence has shed light on their historical reality.

1.4.5 Norse Mythology and the Volva

Norse mythology is rich with tales of gods, giants, and mythical creatures. Among these stories, the volvas held a significant place. They were believed to possess the power of prophecy and were consulted by kings and warriors seeking guidance before important battles or decisions. The volvas were seen as intermediaries between the human and divine realms, offering insights into the future and communicating with the gods.

1.4.6 Archaeological Evidence of Female Shamans in Norse Culture

Archaeological excavations have provided tangible evidence of the existence of female shamans in Norse culture. Burial sites have revealed the presence of women buried with objects associated with shamanic practices, such as staffs, drums, and amulets. These findings indicate that female shamans played a significant role in Norse society and were respected for their spiritual abilities.

1.4.7 The Role of the Volva in Norse Society

The volvas held a unique position in Norse society. They were not only spiritual leaders but also advisors to kings and warriors. Their prophecies and insights were highly valued, and their presence at important events and gatherings was considered essential. The volvas were seen as powerful figures who possessed the ability to communicate with the gods and influence the course of events.

1.4.8 The 9,000-Year-Old Shaman Burial in Bad Dürrenberg

Another remarkable discovery that challenges gender stereotypes in shamanism is the 9,000-year-old shaman burial found in Bad Dürrenberg, Germany. This burial site contained the remains of a female shaman, along with various artifacts and offerings. The presence of a female shaman in such an ancient context provides compelling evidence of the long-standing tradition of female shamanism.

1.4.9 Women as Shamans: Leadership Roles in Ancient Civilizations

The discovery of female shamans in various ancient civilizations highlights the significant roles women played in leadership positions. In societies where patriarchal structures were prevalent, female shamans defied societal norms and emerged as influential figures. They held positions of power and authority, guiding their communities through spiritual practices and providing wisdom and counsel.

The recognition of women as shamans challenges the notion that leadership roles were exclusively reserved for men. It reveals the complex and diverse nature of ancient societies, where women held positions of influence and played vital roles in shaping their communities.

In conclusion, the discoveries of female shamans in history have shattered the gender stereotypes associated with shamanism. The existence of female shamans in Norse mythology, the archaeological evidence of female shamans in various cultures, and the 9,000-year-old shaman burial in Bad Dürrenberg all contribute to a more comprehensive understanding of the diverse roles women played in ancient societies. These discoveries highlight the importance of recognizing and honoring the contributions of female shamans throughout history and challenge us to embrace the wisdom and power of the feminine in shamanic practices.

2

Chapter 2

U**nveiling the Mythical Volva**

2.1 Norse Mythology and the Volva

Shamans, traditionally associated with males, have long been regarded as the spiritual leaders and healers of ancient societies. However, archaeological and scientific advancements have revealed that female shamans played a significant role in ancient cultures as well. These discoveries challenge the prevailing notion that shamans were exclusively male, shedding light on the important contributions of women in spiritual practices throughout history.

The term "shaman" originates from the Tungus people of Siberia, who used it to describe their spiritual leaders. The word itself has its roots in the Evenki language, meaning "one who knows" or "healer." This etymology reflects the central role of shamans as intermediaries between the human and spirit worlds, possessing knowledge and abilities to heal the sick, communicate with spirits, and guide their communities.

In ancient societies, shamans held a revered position, serving as healers, diviners, and spiritual guides. They were believed to possess a unique connection with the spirit realm, enabling them to access knowledge and power beyond the reach of ordinary individuals. Shamans played a crucial role in maintaining the well-being of their communities, providing spiritual guidance, conducting rituals, and offering healing practices.

One fascinating example of female shamans in ancient mythology can be found in Norse culture. Norse mythology features the figure of the Volva, a powerful female seer and shaman. The Volva, often depicted as an elderly woman, possessed the ability to communicate with the gods, foretell the future, and perform magical rituals. While some scholars initially dismissed the Volva as a mythical creation, archaeological evidence has since emerged to support their existence.

Archaeological excavations have unearthed artifacts and burial sites that provide compelling evidence of the Volva's role in Norse society. These discoveries include staffs, amulets, and other ritual objects associated with the practice of seidr, the magical and shamanic arts performed by the Volva. These findings suggest that the Volva held a respected position within Norse communities and played a vital role in religious and spiritual practices.

Another remarkable discovery shedding light on the ancient practices of female shamans is the 9,000-year-old shaman burial in Bad Dürrenberg, Germany. This burial site, dating back to the Mesolithic period, contained the remains of a woman surrounded by an array of ritual objects. The presence of these artifacts, including a headdress made from red deer antlers and various animal bones, suggests that this woman held a significant spiritual role within her community.

The discovery of these ancient female shamans challenges the prevailing narrative that positions men as the sole spiritual leaders in ancient civilizations. It highlights the important role that women played in leadership positions and spiritual practices throughout history. In various ancient civilizations, women held prominent positions as shamans, demonstrating their power, influence, and ability to connect with the spiritual realm.

These female shamans served as healers, diviners, and decision-makers within their communities. They possessed the knowledge and skills to navigate the spirit world, communicate with deities and spirits, and provide guidance and healing to those in need. Their leadership roles extended beyond the spiritual realm, as they often held positions of authority and influence within their societies.

The discoveries of ancient female shamans not only provide a deeper understanding of the past but also challenge the patriarchal narratives that have marginalized women's contributions throughout history. These findings emphasize the importance of recognizing and honoring the significant roles that women played in ancient civilizations, particularly in spiritual and leadership positions.

By acknowledging the existence and influence of female shamans in ancient cultures, we can gain valuable insights into the enduring legacy of women in shamanic practices. These discoveries remind us of the wisdom, power, and spiritual connection that women have possessed throughout history. They inspire us to embrace the feminine aspects of shamanic practices and honor the contributions of women in both ancient and contemporary societies.

2.2 Archaeological Evidence of Female Shamans in Norse Culture

Shamans, traditionally associated with males, have long been regarded as the spiritual leaders and healers of ancient societies. However, archaeological and scientific advancements have shed light on the significant role that female shamans played in various cultures throughout history. This chapter explores the archaeological evidence of female shamans in Norse culture, specifically focusing on the discovery of the mythical Volva and the ancient shaman burial in Bad Dürrenberg.

The Origins of Shamanism and the Role of Shamans in Society

Before delving into the archaeological evidence of female shamans in Norse culture, it is essential to understand the concept of shamanism and the role that shamans played in ancient societies. The term "shaman" originated from the Tungus people of Siberia and refers to a spiritual practitioner who acts as an intermediary between the human and spirit worlds. Shamans are believed to possess the ability to communicate with spirits, perform healing rituals, and provide guidance to their communities.

Shamans held a revered position in society, as they were seen as the bridge between the physical and spiritual realms. They were responsible for maintaining the well-being of their communities, both physically and spiritually. Shamans conducted ceremonies, performed healing practices, and offered divination and prophecy to guide their people. While male shamans have received more attention in historical records, recent archaeological discoveries have revealed the significant role of female shamans in ancient cultures.

The Mythical Volva: Norse Female Shamans

In Norse mythology, the Volva was a mythical female shaman who possessed prophetic abilities and served as a spiritual guide. The Volva played a crucial role in Norse society, providing insight into the future, performing rituals, and acting as a mediator between humans and the gods. While the existence of the Volva was often dismissed as mere myth, archaeological evidence has confirmed the reality of female shamans in Norse culture.

Archaeological excavations have unearthed artifacts and structures associated with the Volva, providing tangible evidence of their existence. These findings include staffs, amulets, and ritual objects that were likely used by the Volva in their spiritual practices. Additionally, runic inscriptions and sagas mention the Volva, further supporting their historical presence.

The discovery of the Volva challenges the notion that shamanism was exclusively a male domain. It highlights the important role that female shamans played in Norse society and their contributions to spiritual practices and leadership.

The Bad Dürrenberg Shaman Burial: A Glimpse into Ancient Practices

One of the most significant archaeological discoveries shedding light on female shamans is the 9,000-year-old shaman burial in Bad Dürrenberg, Germany. This burial site provides valuable insights into the rituals and practices of ancient female shamans.

The Bad Dürrenberg burial contained the remains of a woman adorned with elaborate grave goods, including a headdress made of bird feathers, animal bones, and various ritual objects. The presence of these artifacts suggests that the woman held a high spiritual status within her community and was likely a shaman.

The burial site also revealed evidence of ritualistic practices, such as the arrangement of the body in a fetal position and the presence of red ochre, a substance associated with spiritual ceremonies. These findings indicate that the burial was not merely a burial but a carefully orchestrated ritual, emphasizing the spiritual significance of the deceased woman.

The Bad Dürrenberg shaman burial serves as a testament to the existence of female shamans in ancient cultures and their integral role in spiritual practices. It highlights the importance of recognizing and honoring the contributions of women in shamanic traditions.

Women as Shamans: Leadership Roles in Ancient Civilizations

The discovery of female shamans in Norse culture and other ancient civilizations challenges the prevailing notion that women were marginalized in leadership roles. In many ancient societies, women held positions of power and influence as spiritual leaders and decision-makers.

Prominent female shamans in ancient civilizations, such as the Volva in Norse culture, played a vital role in guiding their communities and shaping their spiritual beliefs. These women were revered for their wisdom, healing abilities, and prophetic insights. They provided a unique perspective and contributed to the overall well-being and development of their societies.

Female shamans were not confined to the role of healers and spiritual guides alone. They often held positions of authority and were involved in decision-making processes within their communities. Their leadership roles extended beyond the spiritual realm, making them influential figures in various aspects of society.

The recognition of women as shamans and leaders in ancient civilizations challenges the patriarchal narrative that has dominated historical accounts. It highlights the importance of acknowledging the significant contributions of women in shaping cultural, spiritual, and societal practices.

In conclusion, archaeological evidence has revealed the existence of female shamans in Norse culture and other ancient civilizations. The discovery of the Volva and the Bad Dürrenberg shaman burial provides tangible proof of the important role that women played in spiritual practices and leadership. These findings challenge gender stereotypes and emphasize the need to recognize and honor the contributions of ancient female shamans. By understanding their roles and significance, we can gain valuable insights into the enduring legacy of women in shamanic traditions.

2.3 The Role of the Volva in Norse Society

The Norse culture is often associated with powerful gods and mythical creatures, but it also had its fair share of fascinating female figures. Among these figures were the Volvas, ancient female shamans who played a significant role in Norse society. The discovery of the Volva and the evidence supporting their existence has shed light on the important role that women played in ancient Norse culture.

2.3.1 Unveiling the Mythical Volva

In Norse mythology, the Volva was a seeress or prophetess who possessed the ability to communicate with the spirit world and gain insight into the past, present, and future. These women were highly respected and sought after for their wisdom and guidance. While the Volva is often considered a mythical figure, archaeological and historical evidence has revealed that they were indeed a part of Norse society.

2.3.2 Archaeological Evidence of Female Shamans in Norse Culture

Archaeological excavations have unearthed artifacts and burial sites that provide compelling evidence of the existence of female shamans in Norse culture. One such discovery is the 9,000-year-old shaman burial in Bad Dürrenberg, Germany. This burial site contained the remains of a woman adorned with ritualistic objects, suggesting her role as a shaman. The presence of these artifacts, such as drums and rattles, indicates her connection to spiritual practices and rituals.

2.3.3 The Role of the Volva in Norse Society

The Volva held a unique and respected position in Norse society. They were sought after for their ability to communicate with the spirit world and provide guidance and insight to their communities. The Volva would often perform rituals and ceremonies, using their knowledge of the spiritual realm to heal the sick, predict the future, and offer counsel to those in need.

The Volva's role extended beyond the spiritual realm. They were also known to be skilled in herbal medicine and were sought after for their healing abilities. Their knowledge of plants and their medicinal properties made them invaluable members of their communities, providing remedies for various ailments.

2.3.4 Rediscovering the Forgotten Female Shamans of Norse Mythology

For centuries, the role of female shamans in Norse mythology was overshadowed by the prominence of male figures. However, recent archaeological discoveries and advancements in scientific research have allowed us to rediscover and appreciate the important role that women played in Norse society.

By examining burial sites, artifacts, and historical texts, researchers have been able to piece together the stories of these forgotten female shamans. These discoveries have challenged the traditional narrative that shamanism was solely a male domain and have highlighted the significant contributions of women in ancient Norse culture.

2.3.5 Female Shamans as Leaders and Decision-Makers

In addition to their spiritual and healing roles, female shamans in ancient civilizations often held positions of leadership and influence. They were respected as wise women who possessed the ability to connect with the divine and provide guidance to their communities. Their role as spiritual leaders allowed them to participate in decision-making processes and shape the direction of their societies.

The presence of female shamans in leadership roles challenges the notion that women were marginalized or excluded from positions of power in ancient civilizations. These women were revered for their wisdom, intuition, and ability to bridge the gap between the human and spirit worlds.

2.3.6 The Enduring Legacy of Women in Shamanic Leadership

The legacy of women in shamanic leadership extends beyond ancient civilizations. The discoveries of female shamans in Norse culture and other ancient societies serve as a reminder of the important role that women have played throughout history. These women defied gender stereotypes and societal expectations, using their spiritual gifts and knowledge to guide and heal their communities.

Today, the legacy of female shamans continues to inspire and empower women who are reclaiming their spiritual heritage. Modern-day female shamans are carrying on the traditions of their ancestors, using their intuitive abilities and connection to the spirit world to bring healing and guidance to those in need.

In conclusion, the discovery of ancient female shamans, such as the Volva in Norse mythology and the 9,000-year-old shaman burial in Bad Dürrenberg, has provided valuable insights into the important roles that women played in ancient civilizations. These discoveries challenge the traditional narrative of male-dominated shamanism and highlight the significant contributions of women as leaders, healers, and spiritual guides. The enduring legacy of female shamans serves as a reminder of the wisdom and power of the feminine in shamanic practices, inspiring women to embrace their spiritual gifts and reclaim their place in the world of shamanism.

2.4 Rediscovering the Forgotten Female Shamans of Norse Mythology

Throughout history, the image of a shaman has often been associated with males, but recent archaeological and scientific advances have revealed that female shamans played a significant role in ancient societies. The discovery of these forgotten female shamans has shed new light on the rich and diverse history of shamanism.

2.4.1 Challenging Gender Stereotypes: The True Meaning of Shamanism

To understand the significance of rediscovering female shamans, it is essential to explore the true meaning of shamanism. Shamanism is a spiritual practice that dates back thousands of years and is found in various cultures around the world. Shamans are individuals who possess the ability to communicate with the spirit world and act as intermediaries between the human and spiritual realms.

The word "shaman" originated from the Tungus people of Siberia, where it referred specifically to male practitioners. However, as our understanding of shamanism has evolved, it has become clear that both men and women held the title of shaman in different cultures. The term "shaman" has now come to encompass all individuals, regardless of gender, who engage in shamanic practices.

2.4.2 The Role of Female Shamans in Ancient Societies

In ancient societies, female shamans held esteemed positions and played vital roles within their communities. They were healers, spiritual guides, diviners, and leaders. Female shamans possessed deep knowledge of medicinal plants, rituals, and spiritual practices, which they used to bring healing and balance to their communities.

The discovery of the mythical Volva from Norse mythology provides compelling evidence of the existence of female shamans in ancient Norse culture. The Volva, also known as seeresses, were powerful women who possessed the ability to communicate with the gods and spirits. They played a crucial role in Norse society, providing guidance, prophecy, and spiritual counsel.

2.4.3 Unveiling the Forgotten Female Shamans of Norse Mythology

Archaeological evidence has further confirmed the existence of female shamans in Norse mythology. Excavations have unearthed artifacts and burial sites that provide insights into the lives and practices of these ancient female shamans.

One remarkable discovery is the 9,000-year-old shaman burial in Bad Dürrenberg, Germany. This burial site contained the remains of a woman adorned with ritual objects and surrounded by offerings. The presence of these artifacts suggests that she held a significant role in her community as a shaman. This discovery challenges the notion that shamanism was exclusively a male domain and highlights the importance of recognizing the contributions of female shamans throughout history.

2.4.4 Female Shamans as Leaders in Ancient Civilizations

The rediscovery of female shamans has also shed light on their leadership roles in ancient civilizations. In many societies, women held positions of power and influence as shamans. They served as spiritual leaders, decision-makers, and mediators between the human and spirit worlds.

Prominent female shamans in ancient civilizations, such as the Oracle of Delphi in ancient Greece and the High Priestesses of ancient Egypt, held immense authority and were revered for their wisdom and spiritual insights. These women played pivotal roles in shaping the religious and cultural practices of their respective societies.

The recognition of women as shamans and leaders challenges the patriarchal narrative that has dominated historical accounts. It highlights the importance of acknowledging the significant contributions of women in shaping ancient civilizations and spiritual practices.

In conclusion, the rediscovery of forgotten female shamans in Norse mythology and other ancient civilizations has provided a more comprehensive understanding of the diverse roles women played in shamanic practices. These discoveries challenge gender stereotypes and emphasize the importance of recognizing and honoring the contributions of women throughout history. By embracing the wisdom and power of the feminine in shamanic practices, we can gain valuable insights and lessons for our modern society.

3

Chapter 3

The Bad Dürrenberg Shaman Burial

3.1 The Discovery of the Bad Dürrenberg Burial

The discovery of ancient female shamans has shed new light on the historical understanding of shamanism. Traditionally, shamans have been predominantly associated with males, but archaeological and other scientific advances have conclusively shown that shamans were both male and female. This revelation has challenged long-held assumptions and expanded our understanding of the diverse roles and responsibilities of ancient female shamans.

To fully comprehend the significance of the discovery of ancient female shamans, it is essential to first understand what a shaman is and where the word originated from. The term "shaman" is derived from the Tungus language of Siberia and refers to a spiritual practitioner who acts as an intermediary between the human and spirit worlds. Shamans are believed to possess the ability to communicate with spirits, perform healing rituals, and provide guidance to their communities.

In ancient societies, shamans held a revered position and played a vital role in the social fabric. They were not only spiritual leaders but also healers, diviners, and advisors. Shamans were sought after for their ability to connect with the spirit realm and provide insights into various aspects of life, including health, agriculture, and hunting. Their wisdom and guidance were highly valued, and they often held positions of influence and authority within their communities.

One remarkable discovery that highlights the existence of female shamans is the mythical Volva from Norse mythology. The Volva, also known as the seeress, was a female shamanic figure who possessed the power of prophecy and divination. While initially dismissed as mere mythological characters, archaeological evidence has revealed the existence of female shamans in Norse culture. The discovery of burial sites containing female remains with shamanic artifacts and symbols has provided concrete proof of the Volva's historical significance.

Another significant archaeological find that has contributed to our under-standing of ancient female shamans is the 9,000-year-old shaman burial in Bad Dürrenberg, Germany. This burial site, dating back to the Mesolithic period, contained the remains of a woman surrounded by an array of ritual objects and artifacts. The presence of these items, including a headdress made of red deer antlers, suggests that the woman held a prominent shamanic role within her community.

The Bad Dürrenberg burial provides valuable insights into the rituals and practices of ancient female shamans. The artifacts found at the site indicate that the woman was involved in healing and spiritual journeys, as well as the performance of ceremonies and rituals. The burial site also suggests that the woman may have served as a spiritual guide and leader within her community, further emphasizing the significant role of female shamans in ancient civilizations.

The discovery of women as shamans has also shed light on their leadership roles in ancient civilizations. Prominent female shamans have been identified in various cultures, including the Siberian Tungus, Native American tribes, and ancient Chinese societies. These women held positions of power and influence, making important decisions for their communities and acting as mediators between the human and spirit realms.

The recognition of women as shamans challenges the prevailing patriarchal narrative that has marginalized and suppressed women throughout history. It highlights the power and influence that women held in ancient societies and the important role they played in shaping their communities. The legacy of female shamans in leadership roles serves as a reminder of the enduring strength and wisdom of women throughout history.

The discoveries of ancient female shamans have not only expanded our understanding of shamanism but also emphasized the importance of recognizing and honoring their contributions. These remarkable women played a vital role in their communities, providing healing, guidance, and spiritual insight. Their wisdom and power continue to inspire and influence contemporary shamanic practices.

In conclusion, the discovery of ancient female shamans has revolutionized our understanding of shamanism and challenged gender stereotypes. The existence of female shamans, such as the Volva in Norse mythology and the woman buried in Bad Dürrenberg, highlights the significant roles they played in ancient societies. These discoveries have not only revealed the diverse responsibilities of female shamans but also emphasized their leadership roles in ancient civilizations. Recognizing and honoring the legacy of ancient female shamans is crucial in embracing the wisdom and power of the feminine in shamanic practices.

3.2 Unraveling the Secrets of the Burial

The discovery of ancient female shamans has shed new light on the historical understanding of shamanism. Traditionally, shamans have been predominantly associated with males, but archaeological and other scientific advances have revealed that shamans were both male and female. This revelation has challenged long-held assumptions and provided a more comprehensive understanding of the diverse roles and responsibilities of ancient shamans.

The term "shaman" originates from the Tungus people of Siberia, who used it to describe their spiritual leaders. The word itself has no gender-specific connotations, yet the prevailing perception of shamans as male has persisted throughout history. However, recent research has shown that female shamans played a significant role in ancient societies, often holding positions of power and influence.

Shamans held a unique place in society, serving as intermediaries between the human and spirit worlds. They were believed to possess the ability to communicate with spirits, heal the sick, and provide guidance and wisdom to their communities. The shaman's role extended beyond mere healing; they were also responsible for divination, prophecy, and conducting rituals and ceremonies.

One remarkable discovery that supports the existence of female shamans is the mythical Volva from Norse mythology. The Volva, often depicted as a wise woman or seeress, played a crucial role in Norse society. She possessed the ability to communicate with the gods and spirits, providing guidance and insight to her community. Archaeological evidence, such as the Oseberg ship burial in Norway, has revealed the presence of female shamans in Norse culture, further confirming the historical reality of the Volva.

Another significant archaeological find that sheds light on ancient female shamans is the 9,000-year-old shaman burial in Bad Dürrenberg, Germany. This burial site, discovered in 1962, contained the remains of a woman surrounded by an array of ritual artifacts. The presence of these artifacts, including a headdress made of bird feathers, a necklace of animal teeth, and various tools and objects, suggests that this woman held a prominent role as a shaman in her community.

The Bad Dürrenberg burial provides valuable insights into the rituals and practices of ancient female shamans. The artifacts found in the burial site indicate that these shamans engaged in healing practices, divination, and spiritual journeys. The headdress made of bird feathers suggests a connection to animal spirits and the ability to communicate with them. The necklace of animal teeth may have symbolized the shaman's power to harness the energy and qualities of different animals.

Interpreting the significance of the Bad Dürrenberg shaman burial requires a deep understanding of the cultural and spiritual beliefs of the time. It is likely that this burial was a reflection of the community's reverence for the shaman and their recognition of her spiritual abilities. The presence of such a burial site indicates that female shamans held a respected and esteemed position within their societies.

The discovery of women as shamans also highlights their roles in leadership positions in ancient civilizations. Prominent female shamans in various cultures, such as the Siberian Tungus, the indigenous tribes of North America, and the indigenous peoples of South America, held positions of authority and decision-making power. These women were not only spiritual leaders but also political and social leaders, guiding their communities in matters of governance and conflict resolution.

The importance of these discoveries cannot be overstated. They challenge the prevailing narrative that positions women as secondary or subordinate in ancient societies. The existence of female shamans demonstrates the power and influence that women held in spiritual and societal realms. It is a testament to the enduring legacy of women in leadership roles throughout history.

The discoveries of ancient female shamans provide valuable insights into the rich tapestry of human history. They remind us of the diverse roles and contributions of women in ancient civilizations and challenge the gender stereotypes that have persisted for centuries. By honoring and recognizing the important role of female shamans, we can gain a deeper understanding of the wisdom and power of the feminine in shamanic practices and embrace a more inclusive and holistic view of history.

3.3 Interpreting the Significance of the Shaman Burial

The discovery of ancient female shamans has challenged the traditional notion that shamans were exclusively male. For centuries, the image of a shaman has been associated with a male figure, but archaeological and scientific advances have shed light on the important role that women played in shamanic practices throughout history. These discoveries have not only expanded our understanding of ancient societies but have also highlighted the significant contributions of women in spiritual and healing practices.

The term "shaman" originates from the Tungus people of Siberia, who used it to describe their spiritual leaders. The word itself has been adopted by scholars to refer to individuals who possess the ability to communicate with the spirit world and act as intermediaries between humans and the divine. While the word "shaman" is of Siberian origin, similar practices and beliefs can be found in cultures around the world.

Shamans held a unique place in society, serving as healers, spiritual guides, and mediators between the human and spirit realms. They were revered for their ability to connect with the unseen forces of the universe and provide guidance and healing to their communities. In many ancient societies, shamans played a crucial role in maintaining the well-being and harmony of their communities.

One remarkable example of the discovery of ancient female shamans is found in Norse mythology. The mythical figure known as the Volva was believed to possess prophetic and magical powers. While some dismissed the Volva as mere legend, archaeological evidence has confirmed the existence of female shamans in Norse culture. Through excavations and analysis of burial sites, researchers have uncovered artifacts and rituals associated with the Volva, providing tangible proof of their role in Norse society.

Another significant discovery that sheds light on the presence of female shamans is the 9,000-year-old shaman burial in Bad Dürrenberg, Germany. This burial site, dating back to the Mesolithic period, contained the remains of a woman surrounded by an array of ritual objects and artifacts. The presence of these items, including a headdress made of bird feathers and various tools associated with shamanic practices, suggests that this woman held a prominent role as a shaman within her community.

The significance of these discoveries goes beyond the mere acknowledgment of female shamans in ancient societies. They challenge the prevailing narrative that positions men as the sole leaders and spiritual authorities. The presence of women in shamanic practices highlights their important roles as healers, spiritual guides, and decision-makers in ancient civilizations.

In many ancient cultures, women held positions of power and influence as shamans. They were respected for their ability to communicate with the spirit world and provide guidance to their communities. Female shamans often served as leaders, making important decisions and offering counsel in matters of governance and community welfare. Their wisdom and spiritual insights were highly valued, and their contributions played a vital role in shaping the social and spiritual fabric of their societies.

The discoveries of women as shamans not only challenge gender stereotypes but also provide a deeper understanding of the diverse roles women played in ancient civilizations. These findings highlight the importance of recognizing and honoring the contributions of women in spiritual and leadership roles throughout history.

The legacy of female shamans in ancient civilizations continues to resonate in modern times. Their wisdom, healing practices, and spiritual insights have left an indelible mark on human history. By embracing and reviving the ancient traditions of female shamans, we can tap into the power and wisdom of the feminine in shamanic practices and bring balance and harmony to our modern lives.

The discoveries of ancient female shamans have opened up new avenues of exploration and understanding. They have challenged long-held assumptions and shed light on the diverse roles women played in ancient societies. By recognizing and honoring the contributions of female shamans, we can gain valuable insights into the power of the feminine and the enduring influence of these remarkable women throughout history.

3.4 The Legacy of the Bad Dürrenberg Shaman

The discovery of ancient female shamans has challenged the traditional notion that shamans were exclusively male. For many years, the image of a shaman has been associated with a male figure, but archaeological and scientific advances have shed light on the significant role that women played in shamanic practices throughout history. These discoveries have not only expanded our understanding of ancient societies but have also highlighted the importance of recognizing the contributions of female shamans.

3.4.1 Challenging Gender Stereotypes: The Role of Female Shamans

Shamans, both male and female, were revered individuals who held a unique position within their communities. The term "shaman" originated from the Tungus people of Siberia and refers to a person who has the ability to communicate with the spirit world and act as an intermediary between humans and the divine. The word "shaman" has since been adopted by scholars to describe similar practices found in various cultures worldwide.

In many societies, female shamans played a vital role in spiritual and healing practices. They were often sought after for their abilities to connect with the spirit realm, perform rituals, and provide guidance and healing to their communities. Despite their significant contributions, the historical records and narratives have often overlooked or marginalized the role of female shamans.

3.4.2 Unveiling the Mythical Volva: Norse Female Shamans

One fascinating example of the rediscovery of female shamans is found in Norse mythology. The mythical figure known as the Volva was believed to possess supernatural powers and acted as a seer and prophetess. While some dismissed the Volva as mere myth, archaeological evidence has revealed the existence of female shamans in Norse culture.

Through excavations and analysis of burial sites, researchers have uncovered artifacts and remains that provide compelling evidence of the Volva's existence. These findings include staffs, amulets, and other ritual objects associated with shamanic practices. The presence of these items suggests that the Volva played a significant role in Norse society, offering spiritual guidance and divination to their communities.

The discovery of the Volva has not only challenged the perception of female shamans but has also shed light on the rich and complex spiritual beliefs of the Norse people. It serves as a reminder that the contributions of women in ancient societies were often overlooked or overshadowed by patriarchal narratives.

3.4.3 The Bad Dürrenberg Shaman Burial: A Glimpse into Ancient Practices

One of the most remarkable discoveries shedding light on the role of female shamans is the 9,000-year-old shaman burial found in Bad Dürrenberg, Germany. This burial site has provided invaluable insights into the rituals and practices of ancient shamans.

The Bad Dürrenberg burial contained the remains of a woman adorned with an array of ritual objects, including a headdress made of bird feathers, a necklace of animal teeth, and various tools associated with shamanic practices. The presence of these artifacts suggests that the woman held a significant spiritual role within her community.

The burial site also revealed evidence of ritualistic practices, such as the use of hallucinogenic substances and the presence of animal bones, which further support the belief that the woman was a shaman. The discovery of this burial site has provided a rare glimpse into the spiritual practices of ancient cultures and highlights the important role that female shamans played in their communities.

3.4.4 Women as Shamans: Leadership Roles in Ancient Civilizations

The discoveries of female shamans have not only challenged gender stereotypes but have also highlighted the leadership roles that women held in ancient civilizations. In many societies, female shamans were not only spiritual guides and healers but also influential decision-makers and leaders within their communities.

Prominent female shamans in ancient civilizations such as the Mayans, Egyptians, and Native Americans held positions of power and respect. They were often consulted for their wisdom and guidance in matters of governance, conflict resolution, and community welfare. These women were seen as mediators between the human and spirit realms, possessing the ability to communicate with deities and ancestors.

The power and influence of female shamans extended beyond their spiritual roles. They were often involved in shaping the social, cultural, and political landscapes of their societies. Their leadership and decision-making abilities were highly valued, and their contributions left a lasting legacy in the ancient world.

The recognition of women as shamans and leaders in ancient civilizations challenges the notion that women were always marginalized or oppressed. It highlights the diversity of gender roles and the significant contributions that women made to their communities.

The discoveries of ancient female shamans, such as the Volva in Norse mythology and the Bad Dürrenberg burial, have provided valuable insights into the spiritual practices and roles of women in ancient societies. These discoveries have not only challenged traditional gender stereotypes but have also emphasized the importance of recognizing and honoring the contributions of female shamans throughout history. By acknowledging the legacy of these women, we can gain a deeper understanding of the rich tapestry of human spirituality and the enduring influence of the feminine in shamanic practices.

4

Chapter 4

W**omen as Shamans**

4.1 Prominent Female Shamans in Ancient Civilizations

Throughout history, the role of shamans has often been associated with males. However, archaeological and scientific advances have revealed that female shamans played a significant role in ancient civilizations. These discoveries challenge the traditional notion of shamans as exclusively male figures and shed light on the important contributions of women in spiritual and leadership roles.

The term "shaman" originates from the Tungus people of Siberia, who used it to describe their spiritual leaders. The word itself has been adopted by scholars to refer to individuals who possess the ability to communicate with the spirit world and act as intermediaries between humans and the divine. Shamans are known for their healing abilities, divination skills, and their capacity to enter altered states of consciousness to gain spiritual insights.

In many ancient societies, shamans held a revered position and played a vital role in the community. They were seen as mediators between the physical and spiritual realms, providing guidance, healing, and protection to their people. Shamans were believed to possess special powers and knowledge that allowed them to communicate with spirits, perform rituals, and navigate the unseen realms.

The discovery of the mythical Volva from Norse mythology provides compelling evidence of the existence of female shamans in ancient times. In Norse mythology, the Volva was a powerful seeress and sorceress who possessed prophetic abilities and deep knowledge of the spiritual world. Archaeological evidence, such as the Oseberg ship burial in Norway, has revealed the presence of female figures associated with shamanic practices. These findings confirm that female shamans, known as Volvas, played a significant role in Norse society.

Another remarkable discovery that highlights the prominence of female shamans is the 9,000-year-old shaman burial in Bad Dürrenberg, Germany. This burial site contained the remains of a woman adorned with shamanic artifacts, including a headdress made of bird feathers and various ritual objects. The presence of these artifacts suggests that she held a high status within her community and performed important spiritual and healing functions. This burial provides valuable insights into the ancient practices of female shamans and their significance in the social and religious fabric of ancient civilizations.

The recognition of prominent female shamans in ancient civilizations challenges the prevailing narrative that positions men as the sole leaders and decision-makers. In many societies, women held positions of power and influence as shamans, guiding their communities and making important decisions. Female shamans were often respected and revered for their wisdom, healing abilities, and spiritual insights. They played a crucial role in maintaining the well-being and harmony of their communities.

In ancient civilizations such as the Sumerians, Egyptians, and Mayans, female shamans held leadership roles and were actively involved in political, religious, and social affairs. They were consulted for their divination skills, healing practices, and spiritual guidance. Female shamans were seen as the embodiment of the divine feminine, representing the nurturing and intuitive aspects of spirituality.

The discovery of prominent female shamans in ancient civilizations highlights the enduring legacy of women in shamanic leadership. These women defied gender stereotypes and societal expectations, asserting their power and influence in spiritual and communal matters. Their contributions paved the way for future generations of women to embrace their spiritual gifts and step into leadership roles.

The recognition of female shamans in ancient civilizations is not only significant for understanding the past but also for inspiring and empowering women in the present. It challenges the notion that women have been historically marginalized and silenced in spiritual and leadership roles. The discoveries of female shamans serve as a reminder of the inherent power and wisdom of the feminine and the importance of honoring and celebrating the contributions of women throughout history.

In the next section, we will explore the power and influence of women in shamanic practices, delving into the various roles they played as healers, spiritual guides, and decision-makers. We will examine the ways in which female shamans utilized their unique gifts and abilities to benefit their communities and connect with the divine.

4.2 The Power and Influence of Women in Shamanic Practices

Shamans, traditionally associated with males, have long been regarded as the spiritual leaders and healers in ancient societies. However, archaeological and scientific advancements have shed light on the significant role that women played in shamanic practices throughout history. The discovery of ancient female shamans has challenged the prevailing notion that shamanism was exclusively a male domain, revealing the power and influence that women held in these ancient traditions.

4.2.1 Challenging Gender Stereotypes: The Role of Women in Shamanic Practices

To understand the power and influence of women in shamanic practices, it is essential to first explore the origins and meaning of the term "shaman." The word "shaman" originated from the Tungus people of Siberia and refers to a spiritual practitioner who acts as an intermediary between the human and spirit worlds. While the term itself is gender-neutral, it has often been associated with male practitioners due to historical biases and patriarchal societies.

In many ancient civilizations, women played vital roles in shamanic practices, serving as healers, diviners, and spiritual guides. They possessed deep knowledge of medicinal plants, rituals, and ceremonies, and were revered for their ability to communicate with spirits and access other realms. These women were seen as conduits of divine wisdom and were sought after for their healing abilities and prophetic insights.

4.2.2 The Mythical Volva: Rediscovering Forgotten Female Shamans in Norse Mythology

One fascinating example of the power and influence of women in shamanic practices can be found in Norse mythology. The Volva, often depicted as wise women or seeresses, held a prominent position in Norse society. They were believed to possess supernatural abilities and were consulted for their prophetic visions and guidance.

Archaeological evidence has provided further support for the existence of female shamans in Norse culture. Excavations have uncovered burial sites containing the remains of women adorned with shamanic artifacts, such as staffs, amulets, and ritual objects. These findings have challenged the notion that the Volva were merely mythical figures, confirming their historical presence and the significant role they played in Norse society.

4.2.3 The Bad Dürrenberg Shaman Burial: Unveiling Ancient Shamanic Practices

Another remarkable discovery that highlights the power and influence of women in shamanic practices is the Bad Dürrenberg shaman burial. This burial site, dating back approximately 9,000 years, provides a rare glimpse into the rituals and beliefs of ancient shamans.

The Bad Dürrenberg burial contained the remains of a woman surrounded by an array of shamanic artifacts, including a headdress made of bird feathers, a staff, and various animal bones. The presence of these items suggests that the woman held a significant role in her community as a shaman. The burial site also revealed evidence of ritualistic practices, indicating the importance of spiritual ceremonies in ancient shamanic traditions.

4.2.4 Women as Leaders and Decision-Makers in Ancient Civilizations

The discoveries of ancient female shamans not only challenge gender stereotypes but also highlight the leadership roles that women held in ancient civilizations. These women were not only spiritual guides and healers but also decision-makers and influential figures within their communities.

In many societies, female shamans were respected and sought after for their wisdom and ability to connect with the spiritual realm. They played crucial roles in resolving conflicts, making important decisions, and providing guidance to their communities. Their power and influence extended beyond the realm of spirituality, shaping the social, political, and cultural landscapes of their time.

4.2.5 The Enduring Legacy of Women in Shamanic Leadership

The legacy of women in shamanic leadership continues to resonate throughout history. Their power and influence have left an indelible mark on ancient civilizations, shaping the beliefs, practices, and social structures of these societies. The recognition of women as powerful spiritual leaders challenges the prevailing narrative of male dominance in ancient cultures and provides a more nuanced understanding of the roles and contributions of women in history.

By acknowledging and honoring the power and influence of women in shamanic practices, we can gain valuable insights into the importance of gender equality and the need to challenge societal norms and stereotypes. The rediscovery of ancient female shamans serves as a reminder of the strength and wisdom that women have brought to spiritual practices throughout the ages, inspiring us to embrace the power of the feminine in our own spiritual journeys.

4.3 Female Shamans as Leaders and Decision-Makers

Throughout history, the role of shamans has often been associated with males. However, archaeological and scientific advancements have revealed that female shamans played a significant role in ancient societies. These discoveries challenge the traditional notion that shamans were exclusively male and shed light on the important leadership and decision-making roles that women held in ancient civilizations.

4.3.1 Challenging Gender Stereotypes: The Presence of Female Shamans

The term "shaman" originates from the Tungus people of Siberia, who used it to describe their spiritual leaders. Over time, the word has come to encompass a wide range of practices and beliefs associated with spiritual healing, divination, and communication with the spirit world. While the word itself may have originated from a specific culture, the concept of shamanism and the presence of shamans can be found in various ancient civilizations across the globe.

In many societies, the role of the shaman was not limited to men. Archaeological evidence and historical accounts have revealed the existence of female shamans in cultures such as the Norse, Siberian, Native American, and African societies. These findings challenge the prevailing assumption that shamans were predominantly male and highlight the significant contributions of women in spiritual leadership.

4.3.2 Female Shamans in Ancient Civilizations: Leaders and Decision-Makers

In ancient civilizations, female shamans held positions of power and influence within their communities. They were not only spiritual healers but also served as leaders and decision-makers. These women possessed deep knowledge of medicinal plants, rituals, and spiritual practices, making them invaluable resources for their communities.

In Norse mythology, the Volva was a mythical female shaman who possessed the ability to communicate with the gods and spirits. Recent archaeological discoveries have provided evidence of the Volva's existence, further solidifying the role of female shamans in Norse society. The Volva played a crucial role in advising leaders, predicting the future, and performing sacred rituals. Their wisdom and guidance were highly respected and sought after, demonstrating the significant influence of female shamans in leadership positions.

Another remarkable discovery that sheds light on the leadership roles of female shamans is the 9,000-year-old shaman burial in Bad Dürrenberg, Germany. This burial site contained the remains of a woman adorned with elaborate ceremonial artifacts, indicating her status as a shaman. The presence of such a burial suggests that this woman held a position of authority and respect within her community, further emphasizing the leadership roles of female shamans in ancient civilizations.

4.3.3 The Power and Influence of Female Shamans

Female shamans possessed unique qualities that made them effective leaders and decision-makers. Their deep connection with the spiritual realm allowed them to access knowledge and guidance that could benefit their communities. Through rituals, ceremonies, and divination practices, female shamans provided spiritual healing, resolved conflicts, and made important decisions for the well-being of their people.

The power and influence of female shamans extended beyond their immediate communities. They often acted as intermediaries between the human and spirit worlds, bridging the gap between the physical and metaphysical realms. This connection allowed them to gain insights into the future, communicate with ancestral spirits, and provide guidance to neighboring tribes or groups.

4.3.4 The Enduring Legacy of Women in Shamanic Leadership

The legacy of female shamans as leaders and decision-makers has left an indelible mark on ancient civilizations. Their wisdom, healing abilities, and spiritual guidance shaped the social, cultural, and political landscapes of their time. The recognition of women in these leadership roles challenges the patriarchal narratives that have dominated historical accounts and highlights the importance of gender equality in spiritual practices.

By acknowledging the significant contributions of female shamans, we can learn valuable lessons about the power and potential of women in leadership positions. Their ability to connect with the spiritual realm, make informed decisions, and provide healing and guidance serves as an inspiration for modern society. It reminds us of the importance of embracing the wisdom and power of the feminine in shamanic practices and beyond.

As we continue to explore and uncover the rich history of female shamans, it is crucial to honor their legacy and ensure that their stories are included in our understanding of ancient civilizations. By doing so, we can celebrate the diversity of human experiences and promote a more inclusive and equitable society.

4.4 The Enduring Legacy of Women in Shamanic Leadership

Throughout history, the role of shamans has often been associated with males. However, archaeological and scientific advancements have revealed that shamans were not exclusively male but also included women who played significant roles in ancient societies. The discovery of ancient female shamans has shed light on their important contributions and the enduring legacy they left behind.

4.4.1 Challenging Gender Stereotypes: Unveiling the Forgotten Female Shamans

The term "shaman" originates from the Tungus people of Siberia, who used it to describe their spiritual leaders. Over time, the word has come to encompass a broader range of spiritual practitioners found in various cultures worldwide. Shamans are individuals who possess the ability to communicate with the spirit world and act as intermediaries between humans and the divine.

In many societies, the prevailing belief was that shamans were predominantly male. However, archaeological evidence and historical accounts have challenged this assumption, revealing the significant presence of female shamans throughout history. These discoveries have shattered gender stereotypes and highlighted the crucial role that women played in ancient spiritual practices.

4.4.2 The Mythical Volva: Rediscovering Norse Female Shamans

One fascinating example of ancient female shamans is found in Norse mythology. The Volva, often depicted as wise women with prophetic abilities, held a prominent position in Norse society. While some dismissed the Volva as mere mythological figures, archaeological evidence has confirmed their existence and their crucial role in Norse culture.

Excavations at various sites have unearthed artifacts associated with the Volva, including staffs, amulets, and ritual objects. These findings provide tangible proof of the Volva's presence and their involvement in spiritual practices. The rediscovery of these forgotten female shamans has allowed us to gain a deeper understanding of Norse mythology and the important role women played in ancient Norse society.

4.4.3 The Bad Dürrenberg Shaman Burial: A Glimpse into Ancient Practices

Another significant discovery that highlights the role of women in shamanic leadership is the Bad Dürrenberg shaman burial. This 9,000-year-old burial site, located in Germany, provides valuable insights into ancient shamanic practices and the prominence of female shamans.

The Bad Dürrenberg burial contained the remains of a woman adorned with elaborate ceremonial attire and surrounded by various artifacts. The presence of these items, such as ritual objects and medicinal plants, suggests that the woman held a high status within her community and played a crucial role as a shaman. This discovery challenges the notion that shamanic leadership was exclusively male and emphasizes the importance of women in ancient spiritual practices.

4.4.4 Women as Shamans: Leaders and Decision-Makers in Ancient Civilizations

The discoveries of ancient female shamans extend beyond Norse mythology and the Bad Dürrenberg burial. Throughout ancient civilizations, women held prominent positions as shamans and spiritual leaders. These women played vital roles in their communities, providing guidance, healing, and acting as intermediaries between the human and spirit realms.

In ancient Egypt, for example, priestesses known as "hemets" served as spiritual leaders and healers. They conducted rituals, interpreted dreams, and provided counsel to the pharaohs and the general population. Similarly, in ancient Mesopotamia, the "entu" were female shamans who held positions of power and influence, advising rulers and performing sacred rituals.

The presence of women in shamanic leadership roles was not limited to specific regions or cultures. From the indigenous tribes of the Americas to the ancient civilizations of Asia and Africa, women played crucial roles as shamans, healers, and spiritual guides. Their wisdom, intuition, and connection to the divine made them natural leaders and decision-makers within their communities.

4.4.5 The Enduring Legacy of Women in Shamanic Leadership

The discoveries of ancient female shamans have had a profound impact on our understanding of ancient societies and the role of women in spiritual practices. These findings challenge the prevailing patriarchal narratives that have marginalized and suppressed women throughout history.

The enduring legacy of women in shamanic leadership serves as a reminder of the power and influence they held in ancient civilizations. Their ability to connect with the spirit world, provide healing, and guide their communities demonstrates the inherent strength and wisdom of the feminine.

Today, as we strive for gender equality and inclusivity, the recognition and celebration of the ancient female shamans' legacy is more important than ever. By embracing their wisdom and power, we can learn valuable lessons about leadership, spirituality, and the importance of honoring the feminine in shamanic practices.

The enduring legacy of women in shamanic leadership is a testament to the resilience and strength of women throughout history. It is a call to revive and honor the ancient traditions that have been suppressed and forgotten. By acknowledging and embracing the contributions of women in shamanic practices, we can create a more balanced and harmonious world that values the wisdom and power of both genders.

5

Chapter 5

The Rituals and Practices of Ancient Female Shamans

5.1 Healing and Medicine

Healing and medicine were integral aspects of the ancient female shaman's role. These powerful women possessed a deep understanding of the natural world and its ability to restore balance and harmony to the human body and spirit. Through their extensive knowledge of herbs, plants, and rituals, female shamans played a crucial role in the physical and spiritual well-being of their communities.

5.1.1 The Shaman's Role in Healing

The ancient female shamans were revered for their healing abilities, which encompassed a wide range of practices. They employed various techniques to address physical ailments, emotional imbalances, and spiritual disharmony. These women understood that true healing required a holistic approach that encompassed the mind, body, and spirit.

Using their extensive knowledge of medicinal plants and herbs, female shamans created potent remedies to alleviate physical ailments. They understood the healing properties of different plants and how to prepare them to maximize their effectiveness. These remedies were often administered through teas, poultices, or ointments, tailored to the specific needs of the individual seeking healing.

In addition to herbal medicine, female shamans also utilized energy healing techniques. They believed that imbalances in the body's energy field could lead to illness and sought to restore harmony through practices such as energy manipulation, laying on of hands, and chanting. By channeling their own energy and connecting with the spiritual realm, these shamans were able to facilitate the healing process.

5.1.2 The Shaman as a Spiritual Guide

Beyond their role as healers, female shamans also served as spiritual guides for their communities. They possessed the ability to communicate with the spirit world and act as intermediaries between humans and the divine. Through their rituals and practices, they sought to gain insight, guidance, and wisdom from the spiritual realm.

One of the primary ways in which female shamans connected with the spirit world was through trance and ecstasy. By entering altered states of consciousness, they were able to transcend the physical realm and access higher realms of knowledge. Through these spiritual journeys, they gained insight into the root causes of illness and received guidance on how to restore balance and harmony.

Divination and prophecy were also essential aspects of the shaman's role. Female shamans used various tools and techniques to gain insight into the future and provide guidance to their communities. These included methods such as reading omens, interpreting dreams, and using divination tools like bones, stones, or cards. By tapping into the spiritual realm, they were able to offer valuable guidance and predictions.

5.1.3 The Shaman's Connection to Nature

Ancient female shamans recognized the profound connection between humans and the natural world. They understood that nature held immense wisdom and healing power, and they incorporated this knowledge into their practices. By observing the cycles of the seasons, the behavior of animals, and the growth of plants, they gained insight into the ebb and flow of life.

Animal spirits and totems played a significant role in the shaman's connection to nature. These powerful beings served as guides and allies, offering wisdom and protection. Female shamans would often invoke the energy and qualities of specific animals during their rituals and healing ceremonies, drawing upon their unique attributes to support and empower their work.

Sacred plants and herbs were also essential tools in the shaman's healing practices. These plants were believed to possess spiritual properties and the ability to facilitate communication with the spirit world. Female shamans would gather and prepare these plants with great care, using them in rituals, ceremonies, and healing remedies.

5.1.4 The Legacy of Ancient Female Shamans in Healing

The discovery of ancient female shamans has challenged the prevailing notion that shamanism was exclusively a male domain. Archaeological and scientific advances have revealed the significant role that women played in ancient societies as healers, spiritual guides, and leaders. These discoveries have shed light on the rich and diverse history of female shamanism, providing a more comprehensive understanding of the ancient world.

The mythical Volva from Norse mythology is a prime example of the importance of female shamans in ancient cultures. Through archaeological evidence and historical accounts, it has been established that the Volva was not merely a myth but a revered figure in Norse society. These powerful women possessed the ability to communicate with the gods, foretell the future, and provide guidance to their communities.

Another remarkable discovery is the 9,000-year-old shaman burial in Bad Dürrenberg. This burial site revealed the remains of a female shaman, adorned with ritual artifacts and surrounded by offerings. The significance of this discovery cannot be overstated, as it provides tangible evidence of the existence and importance of female shamans in ancient times.

The recognition of women as shamans and their roles in leadership positions in ancient civilizations has challenged traditional narratives that have marginalized and suppressed the contributions of women. These discoveries highlight the power and influence that women held in their communities, serving as healers, spiritual guides, and decision-makers.

The legacy of ancient female shamans in the realm of healing and medicine is enduring. Their holistic approach to healing, incorporating physical, emotional, and spiritual aspects, continues to inspire modern healing practices. The connection they fostered between humans and the natural world serves as a reminder of the profound interdependence between all living beings.

In the next section, we will explore the practice of divination and prophecy, shedding light on the insights into the future that female shamans were able to provide.

5.2 Divination and Prophecy: Insights into the Future

5.2 Divination and Prophecy

Divination and prophecy were integral aspects of the practices of ancient female shamans. These gifted women possessed the ability to communicate with the spirit world and gain insights into the future. Through various divinatory techniques and rituals, they sought guidance, foretold events, and provided wisdom to their communities. This section explores the fascinating realm of divination and prophecy in the context of ancient female shamans.

5.2.1 Divination: Seeking Insights into the Unknown

Divination, the art of seeking knowledge of the future or unknown through supernatural means, played a significant role in the practices of ancient female shamans. These wise women utilized a wide range of divinatory techniques to connect with the spiritual realm and gain insights into various aspects of life. Divination was not only a means of predicting future events but also a tool for understanding the present and making informed decisions.

One common method of divination employed by female shamans was the interpretation of dreams. They believed that dreams were a gateway to the spirit world, where they could receive messages and guidance from the divine. These visionary experiences provided them with valuable insights into the future and helped them navigate the challenges of their communities.

Another popular form of divination practiced by ancient female shamans was the reading of signs and omens. They observed natural phenomena, such as the flight patterns of birds, the behavior of animals, or the movement of celestial bodies, to interpret messages from the spiritual realm. These signs were believed to hold significant meaning and were used to guide decision-making and predict future outcomes.

5.2.2 Prophecy: Foretelling the Future

Prophecy, the act of predicting or foretelling future events, was a powerful aspect of the ancient female shaman's repertoire. These gifted women possessed the ability to tap into the cosmic forces and receive visions of what was to come. Through their connection with the spirit world, they could glimpse into the future and provide guidance and warnings to their communities.

The prophecies of ancient female shamans were highly regarded and sought after. Their words carried weight and influenced the decisions of leaders and individuals alike. Whether it was predicting the outcome of a battle, the success of a harvest, or the fate of a community, their insights were considered invaluable.

5.2.3 The Mythical Volva: Norse Female Shamans

In Norse mythology, the Volva were revered as powerful female shamans who possessed the ability to communicate with the gods and foretell the future. These mythical figures played a crucial role in the spiritual and cultural life of the Norse people. While some dismissed the Volva as mere legends, archaeological and historical evidence has shed light on the existence and significance of these ancient female shamans.

Archaeological discoveries have revealed artifacts and burial sites associated with the Volva, providing tangible evidence of their existence. These findings include staffs, amulets, and other ritual objects that were believed to have been used by the Volva in their divinatory practices. The presence of these artifacts suggests that the Volva held a respected and influential position within Norse society.

5.2.4 The Bad Dürrenberg Shaman Burial: Unveiling Ancient Practices

One of the most remarkable discoveries shedding light on the role of ancient female shamans is the Bad Dürrenberg shaman burial. This 9,000-year-old burial site, located in Germany, provides a rare glimpse into the rituals and practices of these ancient women.

The Bad Dürrenberg burial contained the remains of a woman adorned with elaborate ceremonial objects, including a headdress made of red deer antlers and a necklace made of animal teeth. These artifacts suggest that the woman held a significant spiritual role within her community. The presence of these ceremonial objects indicates her connection to the spirit world and her role as a diviner and prophetess.

The discovery of the Bad Dürrenberg shaman burial challenges the prevailing notion that shamanism was predominantly a male domain. It highlights the important role that women played as spiritual leaders and practitioners of divination and prophecy in ancient societies.

5.2.5 Women as Shamans: Leaders and Seers

The discovery of ancient female shamans and their roles in leadership positions within ancient civilizations has shattered the misconception that shamanism was solely a male domain. These women held positions of power and influence, guiding their communities through their spiritual wisdom and prophetic abilities.

In various ancient civilizations, such as the Sumerians, Egyptians, and Celts, women occupied prominent roles as shamans and seers. They were revered for their ability to communicate with the spirit world, provide healing, and offer guidance through divination and prophecy. These female shamans were not only spiritual leaders but also decision-makers, playing a crucial role in the governance and well-being of their communities.

The recognition of women as shamans and leaders challenges the patriarchal narrative that has dominated historical accounts. It highlights the importance of acknowledging the significant contributions of women in ancient societies and the enduring legacy of their spiritual practices.

In conclusion, divination and prophecy were integral aspects of the practices of ancient female shamans. Through various divinatory techniques and rituals, these gifted women sought insights into the future and provided guidance to their communities. The discovery of the mythical Volva in Norse mythology and the Bad Dürrenberg shaman burial have further solidified the existence and importance of female shamans throughout history. These findings have challenged gender stereotypes and emphasized the crucial roles that women played as leaders, seers, and spiritual guides in ancient civilizations. The recognition of the divinatory and prophetic abilities of ancient female shamans serves as a reminder of the wisdom and power of the feminine in shamanic practices.

5.3 Spiritual Journeys

Throughout history, ancient female shamans played a vital role in their communities, serving as spiritual guides, healers, and leaders. While shamanism is often associated with males, archaeological and scientific advances have revealed that shamans were both male and female. This discovery challenges the traditional gender stereotypes surrounding shamanism and highlights the significant contributions of ancient female shamans to their societies.

5.3.1 The Shaman: A Multifaceted Guide

The term "shaman" originates from the Tungus people of Siberia, who used it to describe their spiritual leaders. The word itself has been adopted by various cultures worldwide to refer to individuals who possess the ability to communicate with the spirit world and act as intermediaries between humans and the divine. Shamans are known for their unique ability to enter altered states of consciousness, often through trance or ecstasy, to access spiritual realms and gain insights into healing, divination, and prophecy.

5.3.2 The Role of Female Shamans in Society

Ancient female shamans held esteemed positions within their communities, providing essential services and guidance. They were revered for their healing abilities, spiritual wisdom, and connection to the divine. Female shamans played a crucial role in maintaining the physical and spiritual well-being of their people. They were sought after for their healing practices, which encompassed herbal medicine, energy work, and spiritual rituals.

Moreover, female shamans were not limited to the role of healers alone. They often served as spiritual advisors, mediators, and leaders within their communities. Their wisdom and intuitive insights were highly valued, and they played a significant role in decision-making processes. Female shamans were respected for their ability to navigate the spiritual realms and bring back knowledge and guidance for the betterment of their people.

5.3.3 Unveiling the Mythical Volva: Norse Female Shamans

One fascinating example of ancient female shamans is found in Norse mythology, specifically in the figure of the Volva. The Volva was a mythical seeress and shamanic practitioner who possessed the ability to communicate with the gods and spirits. While some dismissed the Volva as mere myth, archaeological evidence has shed light on the existence of female shamans in Norse culture.

Archaeological findings, such as the Oseberg ship burial in Norway, have revealed artifacts and symbols associated with the Volva. These discoveries provide tangible evidence of the important role female shamans played in Norse society. The Volva's connection to the spiritual realm and her ability to foresee the future made her a revered figure, sought after for her divinatory skills and guidance.

5.3.4 The Bad Dürrenberg Shaman Burial: A Glimpse into Ancient Practices

Another significant discovery that highlights the presence of ancient female shamans is the Bad Dürrenberg shaman burial. This burial site, dating back approximately 9,000 years, offers valuable insights into the rituals and practices of female shamans in ancient times.

The Bad Dürrenberg burial contained the remains of a woman adorned with shamanic artifacts, including a headdress made of feathers, a necklace of animal teeth, and various ritual objects. The presence of these items suggests that the woman held a prominent role as a shaman within her community. The burial site also revealed evidence of ritualistic practices, such as the use of hallucinogenic plants and the presence of animal bones, indicating the importance of animal spirits in shamanic journeys.

5.3.5 Women as Shamans: Leadership Roles in Ancient Civilizations

The discovery of ancient female shamans has shed light on the significant leadership roles women held in various ancient civilizations. These women were not only spiritual guides but also influential decision-makers within their communities. Their ability to connect with the divine and access spiritual realms provided them with unique insights and wisdom that were highly valued.

In ancient Egypt, for example, priestesses held positions of power and authority, serving as intermediaries between the gods and the people. These priestesses, often referred to as "Wab-priestesses," performed rituals, divination, and healing practices. Their role as spiritual leaders and healers was crucial in maintaining the well-being of the community.

Similarly, in ancient Mesopotamia, the role of the "Enheduanna" as a high priestess and poetess exemplified the leadership and spiritual authority held by women. Enheduanna's hymns and prayers to the goddess Inanna were highly regarded and played a significant role in religious and cultural practices.

5.3.6 The Enduring Legacy of Ancient Female Shamans

The discoveries of ancient female shamans have provided a deeper understanding of the important roles women played in ancient societies. These women were not only healers and spiritual guides but also leaders and decision-makers. Their wisdom, intuition, and connection to the divine were highly valued and respected.

The legacy of ancient female shamans continues to inspire and influence modern society. Their practices and beliefs have been passed down through generations, and contemporary female shamans carry on their traditions. By embracing the wisdom and power of the feminine in shamanic practices, we can honor and celebrate the enduring influence of ancient female shamans in history.

5.4 Ceremonies and Rituals

Throughout history, ceremonies and rituals have played a significant role in the practices of ancient female shamans. These sacred acts served as a means for these powerful women to connect with the divine, commune with spirits, and channel their healing and prophetic abilities. In this section, we will explore the various ceremonies and rituals performed by ancient female shamans, shedding light on their profound spiritual significance.

5.4.1 Communion with the Divine

Ceremonies and rituals were essential components of the shamanic practices of ancient female shamans. These rituals provided a sacred space for the shamans to establish a deep connection with the divine and the spiritual realms. Through these ceremonies, they sought guidance, healing, and wisdom from the higher powers they believed in.

One common ceremony performed by female shamans was the invocation of spirits. They would create an atmosphere conducive to spiritual communication, often using sacred plants, herbs, and incense to induce altered states of consciousness. In these altered states, the shamans would enter a trance-like state and communicate with spirits, ancestors, and deities. Through their rituals, they sought to establish a bridge between the human and spirit worlds, acting as intermediaries and conduits for divine messages and healing energies.

5.4.2 Rituals of Healing and Transformation

Healing was a central aspect of the shaman's role, and ceremonies played a vital part in this process. Ancient female shamans would perform elaborate rituals to facilitate physical, emotional, and spiritual healing for individuals and communities. These rituals often involved the use of sacred objects, chants, dances, and energy manipulation techniques.

One such healing ceremony was the purification ritual. The shaman would guide individuals through a process of cleansing and releasing negative energies or spiritual blockages. This ritual aimed to restore balance and harmony within the person's body, mind, and spirit. Through the power of intention and the assistance of spiritual allies, the shaman would facilitate the healing process, helping individuals overcome ailments and achieve a state of well-being.

Another significant ritual performed by female shamans was the initiation ceremony. This ritual marked the transition of an individual into the shamanic path, granting them access to the spiritual realms and the ability to perform shamanic practices. The initiation ceremony often involved a series of tests, trials, and teachings, preparing the individual for their role as a shaman. Through this transformative ritual, the shamanic lineage was passed down, ensuring the continuation of ancient wisdom and practices.

5.4.3 Rituals of Celebration and Connection

Ceremonies and rituals were not solely focused on healing and transformation; they also served as occasions for celebration and connection within the community. Ancient female shamans would lead ceremonies to honor significant events, such as the changing of seasons, harvests, births, and marriages. These rituals were designed to foster a sense of unity, gratitude, and reverence for the natural world and the cycles of life.

One example of a celebratory ritual was the ecstatic dance ceremony. Female shamans would lead the community in rhythmic movements and dances, accompanied by the beat of drums and rattles. Through these dances, participants would enter altered states of consciousness, transcending the boundaries of the physical realm and connecting with the spiritual energies of the universe. This communal experience served to strengthen the bonds within the community and reinforce their connection with the divine.

5.4.4 Rituals of Divination and Prophecy

Divination and prophecy were integral aspects of the shaman's role, and ceremonies were often conducted to seek insights into the future and gain guidance from the spiritual realms. Ancient female shamans would employ various divination techniques, such as scrying, dream interpretation, and the reading of signs and omens.

One notable divination ceremony was the use of sacred objects or tools, such as bones, stones, or cards. The shaman would enter a trance-like state and interpret the messages conveyed through the arrangement or manipulation of these objects. Through this ritual, they would provide individuals with guidance, predictions, and advice, helping them navigate life's challenges and make informed decisions.

In conclusion, ceremonies and rituals held immense significance in the practices of ancient female shamans. These sacred acts allowed them to establish a profound connection with the divine, facilitate healing and transformation, celebrate communal events, and seek guidance through divination. Through their rituals, these powerful women embraced their roles as spiritual leaders, healers, and intermediaries between the human and spirit worlds. The exploration of these ceremonies and rituals provides us with a deeper understanding of the wisdom and power of ancient female shamans.

6.1 Animal Spirits and Totems

Throughout history, shamans have played a significant role in various cultures around the world. Traditionally, shamans were often associated with males, but archaeological and scientific advances have revealed that female shamans were equally prevalent and influential in ancient societies. The discovery of ancient female shamans has shed light on the diverse and essential roles they played in their communities.

The term "shaman" originates from the Tungus people of Siberia, who used it to describe their spiritual leaders. The word itself has been adopted by scholars to refer to individuals who possess the ability to communicate with the spirit world and act as intermediaries between humans and the divine. Shamans are known for their unique abilities to heal, divine the future, and connect with spiritual realms.

In ancient societies, shamans held a revered position and were highly respected for their spiritual knowledge and healing abilities. They served as healers, counselors, and mediators, addressing the physical, emotional, and spiritual needs of their communities. Shamans were believed to possess a deep understanding of the natural world and the interconnectedness of all living beings.

One fascinating example of the discovery of ancient female shamans comes from Norse mythology. Norse mythology speaks of the Volva, powerful female seers who possessed prophetic abilities and were highly respected in their society. While initially considered mythical figures, archaeological evidence has confirmed the existence of female shamans in Norse culture. The Volva played a crucial role in Norse society, conducting rituals, providing guidance, and acting as spiritual leaders.

Another remarkable discovery that highlights the importance of female shamans is the 9,000-year-old shaman burial in Bad Dürrenberg, Germany. This burial site contained the remains of a woman adorned with numerous artifacts associated with shamanic practices. The presence of these artifacts, such as animal bones, suggests that she had a deep connection with animal spirits and totems. This discovery provides valuable insights into the significant role that women played as shamans in ancient civilizations.

The recognition of women as shamans challenges the prevailing gender stereotypes that have often portrayed shamans as exclusively male. These discoveries emphasize the crucial role that women played in leadership positions within ancient societies. Prominent female shamans in various civilizations held positions of power and influence, making important decisions and guiding their communities.

In ancient civilizations, female shamans were not only spiritual leaders but also healers. They possessed extensive knowledge of medicinal plants and herbs, using them to treat ailments and promote healing. The connection between female shamans and the natural world was profound, as they understood the healing properties of plants and their ability to restore balance and harmony.

Animal spirits and totems played a significant role in the practices of female shamans. These spirits were believed to guide and protect the shamans during their spiritual journeys and rituals. Animal spirits were seen as powerful allies, providing wisdom, strength, and guidance. Female shamans would often connect with their animal spirits through trance-like states, allowing them to access the spiritual realm and receive messages and insights.

Totems, on the other hand, were symbolic representations of animals or other natural elements that held special significance for the shaman and their community. Totems served as sources of inspiration, guidance, and protection. Female shamans would often invoke the power of their totems during ceremonies and rituals, seeking their assistance in healing, divination, and spiritual journeys.

The use of animal spirits and totems by female shamans reflects the deep reverence and respect ancient cultures had for the natural world. These practices demonstrate the interconnectedness between humans and the animal kingdom, highlighting the belief that all living beings possess inherent wisdom and spiritual energy.

The discovery of ancient female shamans and their connection to animal spirits and totems provides valuable insights into the spiritual practices and beliefs of ancient civilizations. These discoveries challenge the traditional narratives that have often marginalized the contributions of women in history. By recognizing and honoring the roles of female shamans, we can gain a deeper understanding of the wisdom and power of the feminine in shamanic practices.

6

Chapter 6

The Symbolism and Tools of Female Shamans

6.1 Animal Spirits and Totems

Throughout history, shamans have played a significant role in various cultures around the world. Traditionally, shamans were often associated with males, but archaeological and scientific advances have revealed that female shamans were equally prevalent and influential in ancient societies. The discovery of ancient female shamans has shed light on the diverse and essential roles they played in their communities.

The term "shaman" originates from the Tungus people of Siberia, who used it to describe their spiritual leaders. The word itself has been adopted by scholars to refer to individuals who possess the ability to communicate with the spirit world and act as intermediaries between humans and the divine. Shamans are known for their unique abilities to heal, divine the future, and connect with spiritual realms.

In ancient societies, shamans held a revered position and were highly respected for their spiritual knowledge and healing abilities. They served as healers, counselors, and mediators, addressing the physical, emotional, and spiritual needs of their communities. Shamans were believed to possess a deep understanding of the natural world and the interconnectedness of all living beings.

One fascinating example of the discovery of ancient female shamans comes from Norse mythology. Norse mythology speaks of the Volva, powerful female seers who possessed prophetic abilities and were highly respected in their society. While initially considered mythical figures, archaeological evidence has confirmed the existence of female shamans in Norse culture. The Volva played a crucial role in Norse society, conducting rituals, providing guidance, and acting as spiritual leaders.

Another remarkable discovery that highlights the importance of female shamans is the 9,000-year-old shaman burial in Bad Dürrenberg, Germany. This burial site contained the remains of a woman adorned with numerous artifacts associated with shamanic practices. The presence of these artifacts, such as animal bones, suggests that she had a deep connection with animal spirits and totems. This discovery provides valuable insights into the significant role that women played as shamans in ancient civilizations.

The recognition of women as shamans challenges the prevailing gender stereotypes that have often portrayed shamans as exclusively male. These discoveries emphasize the crucial role that women played in leadership positions within ancient societies. Prominent female shamans in various civilizations held positions of power and influence, making important decisions and guiding their communities.

In ancient civilizations, female shamans were not only spiritual leaders but also healers. They possessed extensive knowledge of medicinal plants and herbs, using them to treat ailments and promote healing. The connection between female shamans and the natural world was profound, as they understood the healing properties of plants and their ability to restore balance and harmony.

Animal spirits and totems played a significant role in the practices of female shamans. These spirits were believed to guide and protect the shamans during their spiritual journeys and rituals. Animal spirits were seen as powerful allies, providing wisdom, strength, and guidance. Female shamans would often connect with their animal spirits through trance-like states, allowing them to access the spiritual realm and receive messages and insights.

Totems, on the other hand, were symbolic representations of animals or other natural elements that held special significance for the shaman and their community. Totems served as sources of inspiration, guidance, and protection. Female shamans would often invoke the power of their totems during ceremonies and rituals, seeking their assistance in healing, divination, and spiritual journeys.

The use of animal spirits and totems by female shamans reflects the deep reverence and respect ancient cultures had for the natural world. These practices demonstrate the interconnectedness between humans and the animal kingdom, highlighting the belief that all living beings possess inherent wisdom and spiritual energy.

The discovery of ancient female shamans and their connection to animal spirits and totems provides valuable insights into the spiritual practices and beliefs of ancient civilizations. These discoveries challenge the traditional narratives that have often marginalized the contributions of women in history. By recognizing and honoring the roles of female shamans, we can gain a deeper understanding of the wisdom and power of the feminine in shamanic practices.

6.2 Sacred Plants and Herbs

Throughout history, ancient female shamans have utilized various tools and techniques to connect with the spirit world and facilitate healing and spiritual guidance. One of the most significant elements in their practices was the use of sacred plants and herbs. These natural substances were believed to possess powerful properties that allowed the shamans to access altered states of consciousness and communicate with the divine.

The Significance of Sacred Plants and Herbs

Sacred plants and herbs played a crucial role in the rituals and practices of ancient female shamans. These plants were considered gateways to the spirit world, enabling the shamans to establish a profound connection with the spiritual realm. The use of these plants was not merely for recreational purposes but was deeply rooted in the belief that they held the key to unlocking hidden knowledge and spiritual insights.

The Origins of Plant-Based Shamanic Practices

The use of sacred plants and herbs in shamanic practices dates back thousands of years and can be found in cultures across the globe. Shamanic traditions have long recognized the profound effects that certain plants have on consciousness and spiritual experiences. These plants were often referred to as entheogens, meaning "generating the divine within," as they were believed to facilitate direct communication with the divine.

The Role of Sacred Plants and Herbs in Shamanic Journeys

For ancient female shamans, sacred plants and herbs served as catalysts for their spiritual journeys. These substances were ingested or used in various forms such as teas, potions, or smoked to induce altered states of consciousness. In these altered states, the shamans believed they could transcend the physical realm and enter the realm of spirits, ancestors, and deities.

Plant Allies and Spirit Guides

Ancient female shamans believed that each sacred plant or herb had its own unique spirit or consciousness. These plant allies were seen as guides and teachers, offering wisdom, healing, and protection during shamanic journeys. The shamans developed deep relationships with these plant spirits, often forming lifelong connections and receiving guidance and knowledge from them.

Examples of Sacred Plants and Herbs

The specific plants and herbs used by ancient female shamans varied across different cultures and regions. Some examples include:

Ayahuasca

Ayahuasca, a powerful plant-based brew, has been used for centuries by indigenous tribes in the Amazon rainforest. It contains a combination of plants, typically including the Banisteriopsis caapi vine and the leaves of the Psychotria viridis plant. Ayahuasca is known for its profound visionary and healing properties, allowing shamans to access deep spiritual insights and facilitate emotional and physical healing.

Fly Agaric Mushroom

The Fly Agaric mushroom, also known as Amanita muscaria, has a long history of use in shamanic practices, particularly in Siberian and Northern European cultures. This distinctive red and white mushroom contains psychoactive compounds that induce altered states of consciousness. It was believed to provide access to the spirit world and was used for divination, healing, and spiritual guidance.

Peyote

Peyote, a small cactus native to North America, has been used by indigenous tribes such as the Huichol and Native American Church for centuries. It contains the psychoactive compound mescaline, which produces profound visionary experiences. Peyote is considered a sacred sacrament and is used in ceremonies for spiritual growth, healing, and connecting with the divine.

Mugwort

Mugwort, a common herb found in many parts of the world, was highly valued by ancient female shamans for its visionary and protective properties. It was often used in rituals and ceremonies to induce lucid dreaming, enhance intuition, and provide spiritual protection. Mugwort was believed to open the doors of perception and allow the shamans to receive messages from the spirit world.

The Importance of Sacred Plants and Herbs in Shamanic Practices

The use of sacred plants and herbs by ancient female shamans was not only a means to access altered states of consciousness but also a way to connect with the natural world and the divine. These plants were seen as allies and teachers, providing guidance, healing, and spiritual insights. The profound experiences facilitated by these substances played a vital role in the shaman's ability to fulfill their roles as healers, spiritual guides, and leaders within their communities.

The discovery of ancient female shamans and their use of sacred plants and herbs has shed light on the diverse and inclusive nature of shamanic practices. It challenges the traditional notion that shamans were exclusively male and highlights the significant contributions of women in ancient civilizations. These discoveries not only enrich our understanding of the past but also inspire a reevaluation of gender roles and the recognition of the power and wisdom of the feminine in shamanic traditions.

6.3 Drums, Rattles, and Other Shamanic Instruments

Shamans, both male and female, have long been associated with the use of various instruments in their spiritual practices. These instruments serve as tools to aid in their connection with the spirit world and to facilitate healing, divination, and other shamanic rituals. Among the most commonly used instruments are drums, rattles, and a variety of other shamanic tools.

6.3.1 Drums: The Rhythm of the Spirit

Drums hold a significant place in the practices of ancient female shamans. The rhythmic beating of the drum is believed to create a bridge between the physical and spiritual realms, allowing the shaman to enter into a trance-like state and communicate with the spirits. The sound of the drum is said to mimic the heartbeat of the Earth, connecting the shaman to the natural world and the forces that govern it.

The drums used by female shamans vary in size and design, reflecting the cultural diversity of these ancient practices. Some drums are small and handheld, while others are larger and played with mallets. The materials used to construct the drums also differ, ranging from animal skins stretched over wooden frames to drums made from clay or other natural materials.

The drumming patterns and rhythms played by female shamans are not merely random beats but are carefully crafted to induce specific states of consciousness. The repetitive nature of the drumming helps to quiet the conscious mind and allows the shaman to enter into a trance, where they can access the wisdom and guidance of the spirit world.

6.3.2 Rattles: Harnessing the Power of Sound

Rattles are another essential instrument used by female shamans in their rituals and ceremonies. These handheld instruments consist of a hollow container filled with small objects such as seeds, stones, or shells. When shaken, the rattles produce a rhythmic sound that is believed to cleanse and purify the energy of the space, as well as to call upon and communicate with the spirits.

The sound of the rattle is thought to have a transformative effect, helping to shift the consciousness of both the shaman and those present during the ritual. The vibrations created by the rattling sound are believed to break up stagnant energy and facilitate the flow of spiritual energy, promoting healing and spiritual growth.

Similar to drums, rattles come in various shapes and sizes, reflecting the cultural traditions of different ancient civilizations. Some rattles are made from animal bones or shells, while others are crafted from wood or gourds. The materials used and the objects contained within the rattles hold symbolic significance, often representing the connection between the physical and spiritual realms.

6.3.3 Other Shamanic Instruments: Tools of the Trade

In addition to drums and rattles, female shamans utilized a wide range of other instruments in their practices. These instruments varied depending on the specific cultural traditions and beliefs of the ancient civilizations in which they lived. Some of these instruments include:

- Flutes: Used to create melodic sounds that evoke a sense of tranquility and harmony, flutes were often played during healing rituals and ceremonies. The haunting melodies produced by the flute were believed to attract benevolent spirits and promote spiritual balance.
- Bells: The ringing of bells was thought to dispel negative energies and summon protective spirits. Bells were often used to mark the beginning and end of rituals, as well as to signal transitions between different stages of the shamanic journey.
- Horns: Horns, often made from animal horns or shells, were used to produce deep, resonant sounds. These sounds were believed to carry the shaman's intentions and messages to the spirit world, acting as a conduit for communication with the divine.
- Chimes: Chimes, made from metal or other resonant materials, were used to create gentle, tinkling sounds. These sounds were believed to attract positive energies and promote a sense of peace and tranquility during shamanic rituals.

These instruments, along with drums and rattles, played a vital role in the practices of ancient female shamans. They served as conduits for spiritual energy, enabling the shamans to connect with the spirit world, heal the sick, and guide their communities. The use of these instruments not only facilitated the shaman's work but also added a sense of sacredness and reverence to their rituals and ceremonies.

The discovery of ancient female shamans and their associated instruments provides valuable insights into the rich and diverse history of shamanic practices. These discoveries challenge the traditional notion that shamans were exclusively male and highlight the important role that women played in ancient societies as spiritual leaders, healers, and decision-makers. By understanding the symbolism and significance of these instruments, we gain a deeper appreciation for the wisdom and power of the ancient female shamans and their enduring influence on spiritual practices throughout history.

6.4 Masks, Costumes, and Ritual Artifacts

Throughout history, masks, costumes, and ritual artifacts have played a significant role in the practices of ancient female shamans. These sacred objects served as powerful symbols, tools, and conduits for connecting with the spirit world and channeling divine energies. In this section, we will explore the fascinating world of masks, costumes, and ritual artifacts used by female shamans in their sacred rituals and ceremonies.

6.4.1 Masks: Portals to the Spirit Realm

Masks held a special place in the rituals of ancient female shamans. These intricately crafted objects were not mere disguises but rather powerful tools that allowed the shamans to embody and channel the spirits they sought to communicate with. Masks served as portals to the spirit realm, enabling the shamans to transcend the boundaries of the physical world and enter into a state of heightened spiritual awareness.

The design of these masks varied across different cultures and regions, reflecting the unique cosmologies and belief systems of each society. Some masks depicted animal spirits, symbolizing the connection between humans and the natural world. Others portrayed ancestral spirits, serving as a bridge between the living and the deceased. The masks were often adorned with feathers, shells, and other sacred objects, further enhancing their spiritual significance.

6.4.2 Costumes: Embodiments of Power and Transformation

Costumes worn by female shamans were not merely decorative garments but rather embodiments of power and transformation. These elaborate and symbolic outfits allowed the shamans to embody the spirits they invoked, enabling them to transcend their human form and access the wisdom and energy of the divine.

The costumes often incorporated elements from nature, such as animal skins, feathers, and plants, symbolizing the interconnectedness of all living beings. They were meticulously crafted, with each element carefully chosen for its spiritual significance. The act of donning the costume was a ritual in itself, marking the shaman's transition from the ordinary world to the realm of the sacred.

The costumes also served as visual representations of the shaman's role and status within the community. They conveyed a sense of authority and respect, signaling to others that the shaman possessed unique knowledge and abilities. In this way, the costumes played a crucial role in establishing the shaman's credibility and influence within the society.

6.4.3 Ritual Artifacts: Tools of the Shamanic Trade

In addition to masks and costumes, female shamans utilized a wide array of ritual artifacts in their practices. These objects served various purposes, from facilitating communication with the spirit world to conducting healing ceremonies and divination rituals.

One of the most common ritual artifacts used by female shamans was the staff or wand. These objects were often adorned with feathers, crystals, or other sacred symbols, imbuing them with spiritual power. The staff served as a conduit for channeling energy and directing the shaman's intentions during rituals.

Another essential tool in the shaman's arsenal was the ritual drum. The rhythmic beats of the drum helped induce trance states and altered states of consciousness, allowing the shaman to journey into the spirit realm. The drum was also used to communicate with spirits and guide the shaman's movements during ceremonial dances.

Other ritual artifacts included sacred stones, amulets, and talismans, each carrying its own unique spiritual significance. These objects were believed to possess protective and healing properties, and the shaman would use them to invoke specific energies or spirits during rituals.

6.4.4 Preserving the Legacy of Masks, Costumes, and Ritual Artifacts

The discovery of ancient female shamans and their associated masks, costumes, and ritual artifacts has provided invaluable insights into the rich and diverse traditions of shamanism. These archaeological findings have challenged the prevailing notion that shamans were exclusively male, highlighting the important role that women played in ancient spiritual practices.

The preservation and study of these artifacts allow us to better understand the beliefs, rituals, and cosmologies of ancient cultures. They provide a tangible link to our ancestors and offer a glimpse into the profound spiritual experiences and practices of the past.

Today, efforts are being made to protect and conserve these artifacts, ensuring that future generations can continue to learn from and appreciate the wisdom and power of ancient female shamans. Museums, research institutions, and indigenous communities are working together to document, study, and display these sacred objects, honoring the legacy of female shamans and their contributions to human history.

In conclusion, masks, costumes, and ritual artifacts were integral to the practices of ancient female shamans. These objects served as powerful symbols, tools, and conduits for connecting with the spirit world and channeling divine energies. The masks provided portals to the spirit realm, while costumes allowed the shamans to embody the spirits they invoked. Ritual artifacts, such as staffs, drums, and sacred objects, facilitated communication with the spirit world and conducted various ceremonies. The discovery and preservation of these artifacts have shed light on the important role of women in ancient shamanic traditions and continue to inspire and educate us about the wisdom and power of the feminine in shamanic practices.

7

Chapter 7

The Spiritual and Mystical Beliefs of Ancient Female Shamans

7.1 Cosmology and the Shamanic Worldview

The ancient practice of shamanism has long been associated with male figures, but recent archaeological and scientific advances have revealed that female shamans played a significant role in ancient societies. The discovery of ancient female shamans has challenged the traditional perception of shamanism and shed light on the diverse roles and responsibilities they held within their communities.

7.1.1 The Shaman: A Multifaceted Figure

To understand the significance of ancient female shamans, it is essential to grasp the concept of shamanism itself. The term "shaman" originated from the Tungus people of Siberia and refers to a spiritual practitioner who acts as an intermediary between the human and spirit worlds. Shamans are believed to possess the ability to communicate with spirits, heal the sick, divine the future, and perform various rituals and ceremonies.

7.1.2 Challenging Gender Stereotypes: The Presence of Female Shamans

While the popular image of a shaman often depicts a male figure, archaeological and historical evidence has revealed that female shamans were prevalent in many ancient cultures. These discoveries have challenged the notion that shamanism was exclusively a male domain and have highlighted the significant contributions of women in spiritual practices.

7.1.3 The Mythical Volva: Unveiling Norse Female Shamans

One fascinating example of ancient female shamans is found in Norse mythology, specifically in the figure of the Volva. The Volva was a seeress and a practitioner of magic, possessing the ability to communicate with the gods and spirits. While some dismissed the Volva as a mythical character, archaeological evidence has provided compelling support for their existence.

7.1.4 Archaeological Evidence of Norse Female Shamans

Archaeological excavations have unearthed artifacts and burial sites that provide tangible evidence of the role of female shamans in Norse society. These discoveries include grave goods such as staffs, amulets, and ritual objects associated with shamanic practices. The presence of these items suggests that female shamans held a respected and influential position within their communities.

7.1.5 The Role of the Volva in Norse Society

The Volva played a crucial role in Norse society, acting as a spiritual guide, healer, and advisor. They were sought after for their ability to communicate with the gods and provide insights into the future. The Volva's wisdom and knowledge were highly valued, and they often played a significant role in important events such as battles, weddings, and funerals.

7.1.6 The Bad Dürrenberg Shaman Burial: A Glimpse into Ancient Practices

Another remarkable discovery that sheds light on ancient female shamans is the Bad Dürrenberg shaman burial. This burial site, dating back approximately 9,000 years, provides a rare glimpse into the rituals and practices of ancient shamans. The grave contained the remains of a woman surrounded by various artifacts, including a headdress made of bird feathers and a variety of tools associated with shamanic practices.

7.1.7 Unraveling the Secrets of the Burial: Rituals and Artifacts

The artifacts found in the Bad Dürrenberg burial site offer valuable insights into the rituals and practices of ancient female shamans. The presence of tools such as grinding stones, animal bones, and plant remains suggests that the woman buried there was involved in healing and divination practices. These findings provide tangible evidence of the important role that female shamans played in ancient societies.

7.1.8 Interpreting the Significance of the Shaman Burial

The Bad Dürrenberg shaman burial holds great significance in understanding the spiritual beliefs and practices of ancient cultures. It demonstrates that female shamans were not only present but also held positions of authority and respect within their communities. The burial site also highlights the importance of shamanic practices in ancient societies and their role in healing, divination, and spiritual guidance.

7.1.9 The Legacy of Ancient Female Shamans in Leadership Roles

The discovery of female shamans in ancient civilizations has challenged the prevailing narrative that positions of power and leadership were exclusively held by men. Prominent female shamans in various ancient cultures, such as the Volva in Norse society, played crucial roles as leaders, decision-makers, and spiritual guides. Their influence extended beyond the realm of shamanic practices, impacting the social, political, and cultural fabric of their communities.

The recognition of women as shamans and leaders in ancient civilizations provides a valuable perspective on the historical contributions of women. It challenges the patriarchal norms that have marginalized women throughout history and emphasizes the importance of gender equality in spiritual and societal realms.

In the next section, we will explore the connection between humans and the spirit world, delving into the beliefs and practices that shaped the shamanic worldview.

7.2 The Connection between Humans and the Spirit World

Throughout history, humans have sought to connect with the spiritual realm, seeking guidance, healing, and wisdom. Ancient female shamans played a crucial role in bridging the gap between the human and spirit worlds. While shamanism is often associated with males, archaeological and scientific advances have revealed that female shamans were equally prevalent and influential in ancient societies.

7.2.1 Challenging Gender Stereotypes: The Role of Female Shamans

Shamans, both male and female, were revered individuals who possessed the ability to communicate with the spirit world. The term "shaman" originated from the Tungus people of Siberia, where it referred to a person who had the power to enter altered states of consciousness and interact with spirits. Over time, the concept of shamanism spread across different cultures and continents, encompassing a wide range of practices and beliefs.

In many ancient societies, female shamans held significant positions of power and respect. They were seen as mediators between the human and spirit realms, capable of healing the sick, divining the future, and guiding their communities. Despite the prevailing gender stereotypes of their time, these women defied societal norms and played vital roles in their communities.

7.2.2 Unveiling the Mythical Volva: Norse Female Shamans

One fascinating example of ancient female shamans is found in Norse mythology. The Volva, often depicted as wise women or seers, were believed to possess supernatural abilities and deep knowledge of the spiritual realm. While some dismissed the Volva as mere mythological figures, archaeological evidence has shed light on their existence and importance in Norse society.

Excavations at various sites in Scandinavia have unearthed artifacts and burials associated with female shamans. These findings provide tangible proof of the Volva's role in Norse culture. The Volva served as spiritual leaders, performing rituals, providing guidance, and acting as intermediaries between humans and the gods. Their wisdom and connection to the spirit world were highly valued by their communities.

7.2.3 The Bad Dürrenberg Shaman Burial: A Glimpse into Ancient Practices

Another remarkable discovery that highlights the significant role of female shamans is the Bad Dürrenberg shaman burial. This 9,000-year-old burial site, located in Germany, offers a rare glimpse into the rituals and practices of ancient female shamans.

The Bad Dürrenberg burial contained the remains of a woman surrounded by an array of artifacts, including animal bones, shells, and ritual objects. The presence of these items suggests that the woman held a special spiritual role within her community. The burial site also revealed evidence of ritualistic practices, indicating that the woman was a shaman who performed sacred ceremonies and connected with the spirit world.

7.2.4 Women as Shamans: Leadership Roles in Ancient Civilizations

The discovery of female shamans in various ancient civilizations challenges the notion that women were solely confined to domestic roles. In societies such as ancient Egypt, Mesopotamia, and the Indus Valley, women held positions of power and influence as shamans and spiritual leaders.

These female shamans played crucial roles in decision-making, governance, and religious practices. They were respected for their ability to communicate with the divine and provide guidance to their communities. The presence of women in leadership positions within shamanic practices highlights the importance of gender equality and the recognition of women's wisdom and power.

The archaeological evidence of female shamans in ancient civilizations underscores the significance of their contributions to society. These women defied societal norms and paved the way for future generations of female leaders and spiritual practitioners.

In conclusion, the discovery of ancient female shamans challenges the traditional perception of shamanism as a male-dominated practice. The existence of female shamans in Norse mythology, as exemplified by the Volva, and the archaeological evidence of the Bad Dürrenberg shaman burial, provide tangible proof of their vital roles in ancient societies. These women served as intermediaries between the human and spirit worlds, providing healing, guidance, and spiritual leadership. Their presence in leadership positions within shamanic practices in various ancient civilizations highlights the importance of recognizing and honoring the wisdom and power of women.

7.3 The Role of Ancestors and Ancestral Spirits

Throughout history, ancient female shamans played a vital role in connecting with the spiritual realm and harnessing the power of ancestral spirits. These wise women understood the significance of honoring their ancestors and believed that they held valuable wisdom and guidance for the living. In this section, we will explore the role of ancestors and ancestral spirits in the practices of ancient female shamans.

7.3.1 Ancestral Spirits: Guardians of Wisdom

Ancient female shamans recognized the importance of their ancestors as guardians of wisdom and ancestral spirits as powerful allies in their spiritual journeys. They believed that these spirits possessed knowledge and experiences that could be passed down through generations, providing guidance and support to the living. By establishing a connection with their ancestors, female shamans sought to tap into this wellspring of wisdom and gain insights into the spiritual realm.

7.3.2 Ancestor Worship: Honoring the Past

Ancestor worship was a fundamental aspect of many ancient cultures, and female shamans played a crucial role in facilitating this practice. They acted as intermediaries between the living and the ancestral spirits, conducting rituals and ceremonies to honor and communicate with their forebears. Through offerings, prayers, and rituals, female shamans sought to maintain a harmonious relationship with their ancestors, seeking their blessings and guidance in various aspects of life.

7.3.3 Ancestors as Protectors and Guardians

Ancient female shamans believed that their ancestors served as protectors and guardians, watching over their descendants and offering guidance and support in times of need. They saw their ancestors as benevolent spirits who could intervene in the human realm, providing protection from malevolent forces and offering assistance in overcoming challenges. Female shamans would often call upon their ancestral spirits during healing rituals, divination practices, and spiritual journeys, seeking their aid in navigating the spiritual realm.

7.3.4 Ancestors as Teachers and Mentors

In the eyes of ancient female shamans, ancestors were not only sources of wisdom but also esteemed teachers and mentors. They believed that their ancestors could impart valuable knowledge and skills, particularly in the realm of shamanic practices. Female shamans would often seek guidance from their ancestors to enhance their healing abilities, refine their divination techniques, and deepen their connection with the spiritual realm. Through dreams, visions, and trance states, ancestral spirits would offer teachings and insights, shaping the path of the female shaman's spiritual journey.

7.3.5 Communing with Ancestral Spirits

Ancient female shamans employed various methods to commune with ancestral spirits. These practices included rituals, ceremonies, and trance states induced through drumming, chanting, or the use of sacred plants. By entering altered states of consciousness, female shamans believed they could bridge the gap between the physical and spiritual realms, facilitating communication with their ancestors. Through these interactions, they sought guidance, wisdom, and blessings from their ancestral spirits, strengthening their connection to the spiritual world.

7.3.6 Ancestors and Shamanic Healing

Ancestral spirits played a significant role in shamanic healing practices conducted by ancient female shamans. These wise women believed that illnesses and ailments could be caused by disruptions in the spiritual realm, and ancestral spirits held the key to restoring balance and harmony. Female shamans would call upon their ancestors to guide them in diagnosing and treating illnesses, seeking their assistance in identifying the root causes of ailments and providing remedies and healing techniques. By working in collaboration with their ancestral spirits, female shamans aimed to restore physical, emotional, and spiritual well-being to their communities.

7.3.7 Ancestral Wisdom and Decision-Making

In ancient civilizations, female shamans held positions of leadership and were often consulted for their wisdom and guidance in matters of governance and decision-making. They believed that their ancestral spirits provided them with insights and perspectives that extended beyond the limitations of the physical world. Female shamans would call upon their ancestors to seek counsel and advice when faced with important decisions, trusting in their ancestral wisdom to guide them towards the most beneficial outcomes for their communities.

7.3.8 The Continuity of Ancestral Traditions

The recognition and reverence for ancestral spirits were not limited to the ancient world but continue to be significant in many cultures today. The practices and beliefs surrounding ancestral spirits have been passed down through generations, ensuring the continuity of ancestral traditions. Contemporary female shamans, inspired by their ancient counterparts, continue to honor and communicate with their ancestors, recognizing the invaluable wisdom and guidance they offer in navigating the complexities of the modern world.

In conclusion, ancient female shamans understood the profound role of ancestors and ancestral spirits in their spiritual practices. They recognized the wisdom, protection, and guidance that their ancestors provided and sought to maintain a harmonious relationship with them. By communing with ancestral spirits, female shamans tapped into a wellspring of knowledge and power, enriching their shamanic practices and benefiting their communities. The enduring influence of ancestral beliefs and practices continues to shape the role of female shamans in contemporary society, highlighting the timeless connection between the living and the spirits of the past.

7.4 The Shaman's Journey

Throughout history, the image of a shaman has often been associated with males, but archaeological and scientific advances have revealed that shamans were not exclusively male. In fact, evidence from various cultures around the world has shown that female shamans played a significant role in ancient societies. This discovery has challenged the traditional gender stereotypes surrounding shamanism and shed light on the important contributions of women in spiritual practices.

7.4.1 Challenging Gender Stereotypes: The Role of Female Shamans

The term "shaman" originated from the Tungus people of Siberia, who used it to describe their spiritual leaders. The word itself means "one who knows" or "healer," emphasizing the shaman's role as a mediator between the human and spirit worlds. While the word "shaman" is often associated with male practitioners, it is important to recognize that female shamans have existed throughout history and across cultures.

In many ancient societies, female shamans held esteemed positions and played vital roles in their communities. They were healers, spiritual guides, diviners, and leaders. Female shamans possessed unique abilities to communicate with spirits, perform rituals, and provide guidance to their communities. Their knowledge of herbal medicine, healing practices, and spiritual ceremonies made them indispensable members of society.

7.4.2 Unveiling the Mythical Volva: Norse Female Shamans

One fascinating example of ancient female shamans is found in Norse mythology. The Volva, often depicted as a wise woman or seeress, held a prominent position in Norse society. While some dismissed the Volva as mere mythological figures, archaeological evidence has revealed the existence of female shamans in Norse culture.

The Volva played a crucial role in Norse society, acting as a bridge between the human and divine realms. They were consulted for their prophetic abilities, providing insights into the future and offering guidance in times of uncertainty. The Volva's connection to the spiritual world was highly respected, and their wisdom was sought after by both leaders and common people.

7.4.3 The Bad Dürrenberg Shaman Burial: A Glimpse into Ancient Practices

Another significant discovery that sheds light on the role of female shamans is the Bad Dürrenberg shaman burial. This 9,000-year-old burial site, located in Germany, provides valuable insights into the rituals and practices of ancient shamans.

The Bad Dürrenberg burial contained the remains of a woman adorned with ritual artifacts, including a headdress made of bird feathers, a necklace of animal teeth, and various tools associated with shamanic practices. The presence of these artifacts suggests that the woman held a high spiritual status within her community and was likely a shaman.

This discovery challenges the notion that shamanism was solely a male domain. It highlights the important role that women played in ancient societies as spiritual leaders and healers. The Bad Dürrenberg shaman burial serves as a testament to the enduring legacy of female shamans and their significant contributions to human history.

7.4.4 Women as Shamans: Leadership Roles in Ancient Civilizations

The discovery of female shamans in various ancient civilizations further emphasizes the significant leadership roles women held in spiritual practices. From the priestesses of ancient Egypt to the oracles of ancient Greece, women played pivotal roles in guiding their communities and connecting with the divine.

In ancient Egypt, priestesses served as intermediaries between the gods and the people. They performed rituals, offered prayers, and provided spiritual guidance to the community. These priestesses held positions of power and influence, demonstrating the recognition of women's spiritual abilities.

Similarly, in ancient Greece, oracles such as the famous Pythia of Delphi were predominantly female. These women were revered for their prophetic abilities and consulted by leaders and individuals seeking guidance. Their words held great weight in decision-making processes, showcasing the significant influence of female shamans in ancient societies.

The presence of female shamans in leadership roles challenges the notion that women were solely confined to domestic spheres in ancient civilizations. It highlights the respect and recognition given to women's spiritual abilities and their integral role in shaping the social and cultural fabric of their communities.

The discoveries of female shamans in ancient civilizations provide valuable insights into the historical contributions of women in spiritual practices. These women served as healers, leaders, and guides, bridging the gap between the human and spirit worlds. Their roles were essential in maintaining the well-being and spiritual harmony of their communities.

The recognition of female shamans and their leadership roles in ancient civilizations is a testament to the enduring legacy of women in spiritual practices. It challenges the patriarchal narratives that have marginalized and suppressed women's voices throughout history. By acknowledging and honoring the contributions of ancient female shamans, we can reclaim and celebrate the wisdom and power of the feminine in shamanic practices.

8

Chapter 8

T he Decline and Suppression of Female Shamanism

8.1 The Rise of Patriarchal Societies and the Suppression of Women

Throughout history, the roles and contributions of women have often been overlooked or marginalized. This is particularly true in the realm of shamanism, where the popular image of a shaman is often associated with a male figure. However, archaeological and other scientific advances have revealed that female shamans played a significant role in ancient societies, challenging the prevailing gender stereotypes.

8.1.1 The Historical Perception of Shamans

To understand the suppression of women in shamanism, it is important to first explore the historical perception of shamans. Shamans are spiritual practitioners who act as intermediaries between the human and spirit worlds. They possess the ability to communicate with spirits, perform healing rituals, and provide guidance to their communities. The word "shaman" itself originated from the Tungusic-speaking peoples of Siberia, where it referred specifically to male practitioners.

8.1.2 The Origins of the Word 'Shaman'

The word "shaman" has its roots in the Evenki language of Siberia, where it originally referred to a male spiritual leader. However, as the concept of shamanism spread across different cultures and regions, the term began to encompass both male and female practitioners. This expansion of the term reflects the recognition of the important role that women played in shamanic practices.

8.1.3 Shamans in Society: Roles and Responsibilities

Shamans held a revered position in ancient societies, serving as healers, spiritual guides, and mediators between the human and spirit realms. They were sought after for their ability to communicate with spirits, perform rituals, and provide guidance in matters of health, divination, and spiritual well-being. In many cultures, shamans were considered the guardians of traditional knowledge and were responsible for maintaining the balance between the physical and spiritual worlds.

8.1.4 Challenging Gender Stereotypes: Female Shamans in History

The discovery of ancient female shamans has challenged the prevailing gender stereotypes associated with shamanism. One notable example is found in Norse mythology, where the mythical figure known as the Volva played a prominent role. The Volva was a female shamanic practitioner who possessed the ability to see the future, communicate with spirits, and perform powerful rituals. Archaeological evidence, such as the Oseberg ship burial in Norway, has provided tangible proof of the existence of female shamans in Norse culture.

8.1.5 The Bad Dürrenberg Shaman Burial: A Glimpse into Ancient Practices

Another significant discovery shedding light on the role of female shamans is the 9,000-year-old shaman burial in Bad Dürrenberg, Germany. This burial site contained the remains of a woman surrounded by an array of ritual artifacts, including animal bones, shells, and stone tools. The presence of these items suggests that she held a prominent position within her community as a shamanic practitioner. This discovery provides valuable insights into the ancient practices and beliefs surrounding female shamans.

8.1.6 Women as Shamans: Leadership Roles in Ancient Civilizations

The discovery of women as shamans in various ancient civilizations challenges the notion that leadership roles were exclusively reserved for men. In societies such as ancient Egypt, Mesopotamia, and the Indus Valley, female shamans held positions of power and influence. They were respected for their spiritual wisdom, healing abilities, and their role as intermediaries between the human and divine realms. These women played a crucial role in decision-making processes and were often sought after for their guidance in matters of governance and community affairs.

The recognition of women as shamans in ancient civilizations highlights the importance of gender equality and the significant contributions that women have made throughout history. It challenges the patriarchal structures that have suppressed and marginalized women's roles in spiritual practices.

In conclusion, the rise of patriarchal societies led to the suppression of women in shamanism. However, archaeological and scientific discoveries have shattered the misconception that shamans were exclusively male. The existence of female shamans, such as the Volva in Norse mythology and the discoveries of ancient shaman burials, has provided undeniable evidence of women's important roles in spiritual practices. These discoveries not only shed light on the historical contributions of women but also emphasize the need to recognize and honor the legacy of female shamans in modern times.

By embracing the wisdom and power of the feminine in shamanic practices, we can create a more inclusive and balanced spiritual landscape.

8.2 Religious and Cultural Shifts

Throughout history, the role of shamans has often been associated with males. However, archaeological and scientific advancements have revealed that ancient female shamans played a significant role in various cultures around the world. These discoveries challenge the traditional notion that shamans were exclusively male and shed light on the important contributions of women in spiritual practices.

8.2.1 Challenging Gender Stereotypes: The Presence of Female Shamans

The term "shaman" is commonly used to describe individuals who possess the ability to communicate with the spirit world and act as intermediaries between humans and the divine. The word "shaman" originated from the Tungusic Evenki language of Siberia, where it referred to both male and female practitioners. This linguistic evidence suggests that from its inception, shamanism recognized the presence of female shamans.

In many ancient societies, female shamans held esteemed positions and played vital roles in their communities. They were healers, spiritual guides, diviners, and leaders. The presence of female shamans challenges the notion that women were solely confined to domestic roles and highlights their significant contributions to religious and cultural practices.

8.2.2 Unveiling the Mythical Volva: Norse Female Shamans

One fascinating example of ancient female shamans is found in Norse mythology. The Volva, often depicted as wise women with prophetic abilities, were revered figures in Norse society. While some dismissed the Volva as mythical beings, archaeological evidence has confirmed their existence and importance.

Excavations at various sites in Scandinavia have unearthed artifacts associated with the Volva, such as staffs, amulets, and ritual objects. These findings provide tangible proof of the Volva's role in Norse culture and their connection to shamanic practices. The Volva served as spiritual leaders, healers, and seers, offering guidance and insight to their communities.

The recognition of the Volva as historical figures rather than mere myths highlights the importance of reevaluating ancient texts and legends to uncover the hidden contributions of female shamans.

8.2.3 The Bad Dürrenberg Shaman Burial: A Glimpse into Ancient Practices

Another significant discovery that sheds light on the presence of female shamans is the Bad Dürrenberg shaman burial. This 9,000-year-old burial site, located in Germany, provides valuable insights into the rituals and practices of ancient shamans.

The Bad Dürrenberg burial contained the remains of a woman adorned with ritual objects and surrounded by various artifacts. The presence of these items, including a headdress made of bird feathers, suggests that the woman held a prominent role in her community as a shaman. The burial site also revealed evidence of ritualistic practices, such as the use of hallucinogenic plants and the presence of animal bones.

This discovery challenges the assumption that male shamans dominated ancient societies and highlights the significant role of women in spiritual and healing practices.

8.2.4 Women as Shamans: Leadership Roles in Ancient Civilizations

The recognition of women as shamans extends beyond individual cases and encompasses various ancient civilizations. Prominent female shamans emerged in cultures such as the ancient Egyptians, Greeks, Celts, and Native Americans, among others. These women held positions of power and influence, serving as spiritual leaders, healers, and advisors.

In ancient Egypt, for example, priestesses known as "hemets" played a crucial role in religious ceremonies and healing practices. They were revered for their ability to communicate with the gods and provide guidance to their communities. Similarly, in ancient Greece, the Oracle of Delphi, a female priestess, served as a conduit between the mortal and divine realms, offering prophecies and advice.

The presence of female shamans in leadership roles challenges the notion that women were excluded from positions of power in ancient societies. These women played vital roles in shaping religious and cultural practices, and their influence extended beyond the spiritual realm.

The recognition of women as shamans in ancient civilizations provides a more comprehensive understanding of the diverse roles women played in shaping society and challenges the patriarchal narratives that have marginalized their contributions.

8.3 The Legacy of Female Shamanism in Modern Times

8.3 The Legacy of Female Shamanism in Modern Times

Throughout history, the role of shamans has often been associated with males. However, archaeological and scientific advancements have revealed that shamans were not exclusively male but also included powerful and revered female practitioners. The discovery of ancient female shamans has shed light on the significant contributions they made to their communities and the enduring legacy they have left behind.

8.3.1 Challenging Gender Stereotypes: The Presence of Female Shamans

The term "shaman" is commonly used to describe a spiritual healer or guide who acts as an intermediary between the human and spirit worlds. The word "shaman" originated from the Tungus people of Siberia, where it referred specifically to male practitioners. However, as research has shown, the practice of shamanism was not limited to one gender.

Archaeological evidence from various cultures around the world has revealed the existence of female shamans. These discoveries challenge the prevailing notion that shamans were exclusively male. In fact, many ancient societies recognized and revered the unique abilities and spiritual power of women, allowing them to take on the role of shamans.

8.3.2 The Role of Female Shamans in Society

Female shamans played vital roles within their communities, serving as healers, spiritual guides, and leaders. They possessed deep knowledge of medicinal plants, rituals, and spiritual practices, which they utilized to bring about healing, maintain harmony, and provide guidance to their people.

In many ancient civilizations, female shamans held positions of authority and respect. They were often consulted for their wisdom and insight, not only in matters of health and well-being but also in decision-making processes. Their ability to communicate with the spirit world and access higher realms of consciousness made them valuable assets to their communities.

8.3.3 Unveiling the Mythical Volva: Norse Female Shamans

One fascinating example of ancient female shamans is found in Norse mythology. The Volva, also known as the Völva or Vǫlva, were powerful seers and practitioners of magic. They were believed to possess the ability to communicate with the gods and spirits, foretell the future, and influence the course of events.

Archaeological evidence has provided insights into the existence of Volva in Norse society. The discovery of burial sites containing the remains of women buried with shamanic artifacts and symbols suggests that the Volva were not merely mythical figures but real women who held significant spiritual and societal roles.

8.3.4 The Bad Dürrenberg Shaman Burial: A Glimpse into Ancient Practices

Another remarkable discovery that highlights the presence of female shamans is the Bad Dürrenberg shaman burial. This burial site, dating back approximately 9,000 years, provides valuable insights into the rituals and practices of ancient female shamans.

The Bad Dürrenberg burial contained the remains of a woman surrounded by various artifacts associated with shamanic practices. These artifacts included a headdress made of bird feathers, a necklace made of animal teeth, and a collection of medicinal plants. The presence of these items suggests that the woman buried at Bad Dürrenberg held a significant role as a shaman within her community.

8.3.5 Women as Shamans: Leadership Roles in Ancient Civilizations

The discovery of female shamans in ancient civilizations highlights the important leadership roles they held. Women in these positions not only served as spiritual guides and healers but also as decision-makers and influencers within their communities.

Prominent female shamans in ancient civilizations, such as the Volva in Norse society, held considerable power and influence. They were respected for their abilities to communicate with the spirit world and provide guidance in matters of great importance. Their leadership roles extended beyond the realm of spirituality, as they often played key roles in political and social decision-making processes.

8.3.6 The Legacy of Female Shamanism in Modern Times

The legacy of female shamanism continues to resonate in modern times. The recognition and understanding of the significant contributions made by ancient female shamans have paved the way for a reevaluation of gender roles and the importance of feminine wisdom and power.

The discoveries of ancient female shamans have challenged the patriarchal narratives that have marginalized women throughout history. They have provided a historical precedent for the inclusion of women in spiritual leadership roles and have inspired contemporary women to reclaim their ancestral wisdom and spiritual practices.

By acknowledging and honoring the legacy of female shamans, we can embrace a more balanced and inclusive approach to spirituality and leadership. The wisdom and power of the feminine, as exemplified by ancient female shamans, can serve as a guiding light in our modern world, reminding us of the importance of nurturing our connection with the natural world, embracing our intuitive abilities, and honoring the sacredness of all life.

In the next chapter, we will explore the practices and beliefs of contemporary female shamans, examining how they carry on the traditions of their ancient predecessors and the impact they have on the global spiritual landscape.

8.4 Reviving and Honoring the Ancient Female Shamanic Traditions

Throughout history, the role of shamans has often been associated with males. However, archaeological and scientific advancements have revealed that ancient female shamans played a significant role in societies around the world. These discoveries have challenged the traditional narrative and shed light on the important contributions of women in shamanic practices.

8.4.1 Challenging Gender Stereotypes: Rediscovering Ancient Female Shamans

The term "shaman" is commonly used to describe individuals who possess spiritual and healing abilities, acting as intermediaries between the human and spirit worlds. The word "shaman" originated from the Tungus people of Siberia, where it referred specifically to male practitioners. However, as research has shown, the concept of shamanism and its practitioners were not limited to a specific gender.

8.4.2 The Role of Female Shamans in Society

Ancient female shamans held esteemed positions within their communities, serving as healers, spiritual guides, and leaders. They played a vital role in maintaining the physical and spiritual well-being of their people. These women possessed deep knowledge of medicinal plants, rituals, and divination practices, which they utilized to bring healing and guidance to their communities.

8.4.3 Unveiling the Mythical Volva: Norse Female Shamans

One fascinating example of ancient female shamans is found in Norse mythology, specifically the figure known as the Volva. The Volva was a seeress and a practitioner of magic, possessing the ability to communicate with the gods and spirits. While some dismissed the Volva as a mythical character, archaeological evidence has confirmed the existence of female shamans in Norse culture.

8.4.4 Archaeological Evidence: Rediscovering the Forgotten Female Shamans

Archaeological discoveries have provided valuable insights into the existence of female shamans throughout history. One such discovery is the 9,000-year-old shaman burial in Bad Dürrenberg, Germany. This burial site contained the remains of a woman adorned with ritual artifacts, suggesting her role as a shaman. The presence of such burials highlights the significance of women in ancient shamanic practices.

8.4.5 Women as Shamans: Leadership Roles in Ancient Civilizations

The discovery of female shamans also reveals their prominent roles as leaders in ancient civilizations. These women held positions of power and influence, making important decisions for their communities. They were respected for their wisdom, spiritual insights, and ability to connect with the divine. The existence of female shamans challenges the notion that women were solely confined to domestic roles in ancient societies.

8.4.6 The Enduring Legacy of Women in Shamanic Leadership

The legacy of women in shamanic leadership continues to resonate in modern times. The recognition of ancient female shamans and their leadership roles serves as a reminder of the inherent power and wisdom of women. By acknowledging and honoring this legacy, we can reclaim and revitalize the ancient traditions of female shamanism.

8.4.7 Reviving Ancient Female Shamanic Traditions

In recent years, there has been a growing interest in reviving and honoring the ancient traditions of female shamans. This resurgence aims to reclaim the lost knowledge and practices of women in shamanic roles. Through research, education, and the sharing of ancestral wisdom, efforts are being made to revive and preserve the ancient female shamanic traditions.

8.4.8 Honoring the Wisdom of the Feminine

Reviving the ancient female shamanic traditions involves recognizing and honoring the wisdom of the feminine. It is an acknowledgment of the unique perspectives, intuitive abilities, and nurturing qualities that women bring to shamanic practices. By embracing the wisdom of the feminine, we can create a more balanced and inclusive approach to spirituality and healing.

8.4.9 Preserving and Passing Down Knowledge

Preserving and passing down the knowledge of ancient female shamans is crucial for the continuation of these traditions. Efforts are being made to document and record the practices, rituals, and wisdom of female shamans from various cultures. This ensures that future generations can learn from and build upon the rich heritage of female shamanism.

8.4.10 Embracing Diversity and Inclusivity

Reviving and honoring the ancient female shamanic traditions also involves embracing diversity and inclusivity. It is essential to recognize that female shamans existed in various cultures and regions, each with their unique practices and beliefs. By embracing this diversity, we can foster a more inclusive and respectful approach to shamanic traditions.

In conclusion, the discovery of ancient female shamans has challenged the traditional narrative that shamanism was solely a male domain. Archaeological and scientific advancements have revealed the significant roles that women played as healers, spiritual guides, and leaders in ancient societies. By reviving and honoring the ancient female shamanic traditions, we can reclaim the wisdom and power of the feminine and create a more inclusive and balanced approach to spirituality and healing.

9

Chapter 9

Contemporary Female Shamans

9.1 Modern-Day Female Shamans

Throughout history, the role of shamans has often been associated with males. However, archaeological and scientific advances have revealed that ancient female shamans played a significant role in societies around the world. These discoveries challenge the traditional notion that shamans were exclusively male and shed light on the important contributions of women in spiritual practices.

9.1.1 Challenging Gender Stereotypes: The Role of Female Shamans

The term "shaman" originates from the Tungus people of Siberia, who used it to describe their spiritual leaders. The word "shaman" has since been adopted by scholars to refer to individuals who possess the ability to communicate with the spirit world and act as intermediaries between humans and the divine. While the word itself may have originated from a male-centric culture, the role of shamans was not limited to men.

In many ancient societies, female shamans held positions of power and influence. They were revered for their ability to connect with the spiritual realm and were sought after for their healing and divination skills. These women played a crucial role in their communities, providing guidance, performing rituals, and acting as mediators between the physical and spiritual realms.

9.1.2 Unveiling the Mythical Volva: Norse Female Shamans

One fascinating example of ancient female shamans is found in Norse mythology. The Volva, often depicted as wise women or seers, held a prominent position in Norse society. While some dismissed the Volva as mere mythological figures, archaeological evidence has confirmed their existence and shed light on their important role.

Excavations at various sites in Scandinavia have uncovered artifacts associated with the Volva, including staffs, amulets, and ritual objects. These findings provide tangible evidence of the Volva's presence and their involvement in spiritual practices. The Volva were highly respected and sought after for their ability to communicate with the gods, perform divination, and provide guidance to their communities.

9.1.3 The Bad Dürrenberg Shaman Burial: A Glimpse into Ancient Practices

In recent years, the discovery of the Bad Dürrenberg shaman burial in Germany has further highlighted the significant role of female shamans in ancient societies. This burial, dating back approximately 9,000 years, provides a rare glimpse into the rituals and practices of ancient female shamans.

The Bad Dürrenberg burial site contained the remains of a woman surrounded by an array of artifacts, including animal bones, shells, and ritual objects. The presence of these items suggests that the woman held a special spiritual role within her community. The burial site also revealed evidence of ritualistic practices, indicating that the woman was likely a shaman who performed sacred ceremonies and acted as a spiritual guide.

9.1.4 Women as Shamans: Leadership Roles in Ancient Civilizations

The discovery of ancient female shamans challenges the notion that women were marginalized in ancient societies. In fact, women held prominent leadership roles in many ancient civilizations, and their influence extended beyond the realm of spiritual practices.

Prominent female shamans in ancient civilizations, such as the Oracle of Delphi in ancient Greece or the priestesses of ancient Egypt, held positions of power and authority. These women were not only spiritual leaders but also decision-makers and advisors to rulers. Their wisdom and guidance were highly valued, and they played a crucial role in shaping the political, social, and religious landscape of their respective societies.

9.1.5 The Legacy of Ancient Female Shamans

The discoveries of ancient female shamans have had a profound impact on our understanding of ancient societies and the role of women within them. These findings challenge the patriarchal narratives that have dominated historical accounts and highlight the significant contributions of women in spiritual practices and leadership roles.

The legacy of ancient female shamans continues to inspire and empower women in contemporary society. Today, there is a growing movement of modern-day female shamans who draw inspiration from their ancient counterparts. These women embrace the wisdom and power of the feminine in shamanic practices, providing healing, guidance, and spiritual support to individuals and communities.

In conclusion, the discovery of ancient female shamans has shattered gender stereotypes and revealed the important role women played in spiritual practices and leadership roles in ancient civilizations. The recognition of these women as powerful spiritual figures challenges the patriarchal narratives that have marginalized women throughout history. The legacy of ancient female shamans continues to inspire and empower women in modern times, as they carry on the traditions and wisdom of their ancestors.

9.2 The Challenges and Opportunities for Female Shamans Today

Throughout history, the role of shamans has often been associated with males. However, archaeological and scientific advances have revealed that shamans were not exclusively male but also included females. This discovery challenges the traditional gender stereotypes surrounding shamanism and highlights the important contributions of ancient female shamans. In contemporary society, female shamans face both challenges and opportunities as they continue to carry on the ancient traditions.

9.2.1 Challenging Gender Stereotypes: The Role of Female Shamans

The word "shaman" originates from the Tungus language of Siberia, where it refers to a person who has the ability to communicate with the spirit world and act as an intermediary between humans and the divine. Traditionally, shamans were believed to possess supernatural powers and were highly respected members of their communities. While the term "shaman" is often associated with male practitioners, it is important to recognize that female shamans have played a significant role throughout history.

In many ancient societies, female shamans held positions of power and influence. They were healers, spiritual guides, and leaders within their communities. The discovery of the mythical Volva from Norse mythology provides evidence of the existence of female shamans in ancient cultures. The Volva, also known as seeresses, were revered for their prophetic abilities and their connection to the spirit world. Archaeological evidence supports the existence of female shamans in Norse society, challenging the notion that shamanism was solely a male domain.

9.2.2 The Discovery of Ancient Female Shaman Burials

One remarkable archaeological discovery that sheds light on the role of female shamans is the 9,000-year-old shaman burial in Bad Dürrenberg, Germany. This burial site provides valuable insights into the rituals and practices of ancient female shamans. The grave contained the remains of a woman adorned with elaborate jewelry and surrounded by various artifacts, including a headdress made of bird feathers and a staff adorned with carved animal figures.

The significance of this burial lies in the recognition of the woman's role as a shaman within her community. The presence of ceremonial objects suggests that she held a position of spiritual authority and performed important rituals. This discovery challenges the notion that female shamans were marginalized or overlooked in ancient societies. Instead, it highlights their integral role in religious and spiritual practices.

9.2.3 Female Shamans as Leaders in Ancient Civilizations

In addition to their spiritual and healing roles, female shamans often held leadership positions within their communities. Prominent female shamans in ancient civilizations, such as the Oracle of Delphi in ancient Greece or the High Priestesses of ancient Egypt, wielded significant power and influence. These women were not only revered for their spiritual abilities but also sought after for their wisdom and guidance in matters of governance and decision-making.

The power and influence of female shamans extended beyond their immediate communities. They often acted as mediators in conflicts, healers in times of illness, and advisors to rulers. Their ability to connect with the spirit world and access divine knowledge made them invaluable assets in ancient societies. The legacy of these female shamans can still be felt today, as their contributions continue to inspire and shape our understanding of leadership and spirituality.

9.2.4 Challenges and Opportunities for Female Shamans Today

While the recognition of female shamans in ancient history is a significant step towards gender equality in spiritual practices, contemporary female shamans still face challenges in their roles. In some cultures, traditional gender roles and societal expectations may limit the opportunities available to women in shamanic practices. However, there are also numerous opportunities for female shamans to thrive and make a meaningful impact in today's world.

One of the challenges faced by female shamans today is the need to navigate patriarchal structures and overcome gender biases. Breaking free from the historical marginalization of women in spiritual leadership roles requires perseverance and a commitment to challenging societal norms. Female shamans must assert their legitimacy and expertise in the face of skepticism and prejudice.

On the other hand, the increasing recognition and acceptance of diverse spiritual practices present opportunities for female shamans to share their wisdom and healing abilities with a wider audience. As society becomes more open to alternative healing modalities and spiritual beliefs, female shamans can find a supportive community that values their unique contributions. The internet and social media platforms also provide avenues for female shamans to connect with like-minded individuals and share their knowledge on a global scale.

In conclusion, the challenges and opportunities for female shamans today are intertwined with the ongoing struggle for gender equality and the recognition of women's contributions throughout history. By embracing their roles as healers, spiritual guides, and leaders, female shamans can continue to inspire and empower others, just as their ancient counterparts did. The journey towards equality and acceptance may be challenging, but the enduring legacy of ancient female shamans serves as a powerful reminder of the strength and resilience of women in shamanic practices.

9.3 Female Shamans as Healers and Spiritual Guides

Throughout history, the role of shamans has often been associated with males. However, archaeological and other scientific advances have revealed that shamans were not exclusively male but also included females. The discovery of ancient female shamans has provided valuable insights into the diverse and complex nature of shamanic practices across different cultures and time periods.

The Meaning and Origins of Shamanism

Before delving into the role of female shamans, it is important to understand what a shaman is and where the word originated from. The term "shaman" is derived from the Tungus language of Siberia and refers to a person who has the ability to communicate with the spirit world and act as an intermediary between the human and spiritual realms. Shamans are believed to possess special powers and knowledge that enable them to heal the sick, divine the future, and perform various rituals and ceremonies.

Shamans in Society: Roles and Responsibilities

Shamans played significant roles in their respective societies, serving as healers, spiritual guides, and mediators between humans and the spirit world. They were often sought after for their abilities to cure illnesses, provide spiritual guidance, and perform rituals for various purposes such as fertility, protection, and prosperity. In many cultures, shamans were highly respected and held positions of authority and influence within their communities.

Unveiling the Mythical Volva: Norse Female Shamans

One fascinating example of ancient female shamans is found in Norse mythology, specifically the figure known as the Volva. The Volva was a mythical seeress and shamanic practitioner who possessed the ability to communicate with the gods and spirits. While initially considered a mythical character, archaeological evidence has shed light on the existence of female shamans in Norse culture.

Archaeological findings, such as the Oseberg ship burial in Norway, have revealed the presence of women buried with shamanic tools and artifacts, suggesting their role as spiritual leaders and healers. These discoveries have challenged the notion that female shamans were merely products of myth and folklore, highlighting their significant contributions to Norse society.

The Bad Dürrenberg Shaman Burial: A Glimpse into Ancient Practices

Another remarkable discovery that provides insight into the role of female shamans is the 9,000-year-old shaman burial in Bad Dürrenberg, Germany. This burial site contained the remains of a woman adorned with elaborate jewelry and surrounded by various ritual objects. The presence of these artifacts suggests that she held a prominent position within her community as a shamanic practitioner.

The Bad Dürrenberg burial offers a rare glimpse into the ancient practices and rituals performed by female shamans. It demonstrates the importance of these women in their societies and their role as healers and spiritual guides. The discovery of such burials underscores the significance of recognizing and honoring the contributions of female shamans throughout history.

Women as Shamans: Leadership Roles in Ancient Civilizations

The discovery of ancient female shamans also highlights their leadership roles in ancient civilizations. In many societies, women held positions of power and influence as shamans, making important decisions and guiding their communities. Prominent female shamans in ancient civilizations, such as the Oracle of Delphi in ancient Greece and the High Priestesses of ancient Egypt, played crucial roles in religious and political affairs.

These women not only served as spiritual guides but also acted as advisors to rulers and decision-makers. Their wisdom, intuition, and connection to the spirit world were highly valued, and their leadership roles were integral to the functioning of their societies.

Female Shamans as Healers and Spiritual Guides

One of the primary roles of female shamans was that of healers. They possessed extensive knowledge of medicinal plants, herbs, and healing techniques, which they used to treat various ailments and diseases. Female shamans were skilled in diagnosing illnesses, performing rituals, and administering remedies to restore balance and harmony to the body, mind, and spirit.

As spiritual guides, female shamans facilitated the spiritual growth and development of individuals within their communities. They provided guidance, performed divination and prophecy, and conducted ceremonies and rituals to connect individuals with the divine and the spirit world. Female shamans were seen as intermediaries between humans and the spiritual realm, helping individuals navigate their spiritual journeys and seek answers to life's mysteries.

The healing and spiritual guidance provided by female shamans were essential for the well-being and overall harmony of their communities. Their abilities to heal physical and spiritual ailments were highly valued and sought after, making them indispensable members of society.

In conclusion, the discovery of ancient female shamans has challenged the traditional perception of shamans as exclusively male. These women played vital roles as healers and spiritual guides, providing invaluable services to their communities. The archaeological evidence of female shamans in Norse mythology and the 9,000-year-old shaman burial in Bad Dürrenberg highlight the importance of recognizing and honoring the contributions of women in shamanic practices. Furthermore, the leadership roles of women in ancient civilizations demonstrate the enduring legacy of female shamans in history. Their roles as healers and spiritual guides were integral to the well-being and spiritual growth of their communities, making them invaluable figures in ancient societies.

9.4 The Global Impact of Contemporary Female Shamanism

Throughout history, the role of shamans has often been associated with males. However, archaeological and other scientific advances have revealed that shamans were not exclusively male, but also included powerful and revered female practitioners. The discovery of ancient female shamans has challenged traditional gender stereotypes and shed light on the significant contributions of women in spiritual and healing practices.

9.4.1 Challenging Gender Stereotypes: The Presence of Female Shamans

The term "shaman" is commonly used to describe a spiritual healer or guide who acts as an intermediary between the human and spirit realms. The word "shaman" originated from the Tungus people of Siberia, where it referred specifically to male practitioners. However, as research has expanded, it has become evident that female shamans existed in various cultures worldwide.

9.4.2 The Role of Female Shamans in Society

Female shamans played vital roles within their communities, providing spiritual guidance, healing, and divination. They were often seen as mediators between the physical and spiritual realms, possessing the ability to communicate with spirits, ancestors, and deities. Their practices encompassed a wide range of responsibilities, including healing the sick, performing rituals, and offering guidance in matters of daily life.

9.4.3 Unveiling the Mythical Volva: Norse Female Shamans

One fascinating example of ancient female shamans is found in Norse mythology. The Volva, often depicted as wise women or seers, held significant influence within Norse society. They possessed the ability to communicate with the gods and spirits, providing guidance and prophetic insights. While some dismissed the Volva as mere mythological figures, archaeological evidence has confirmed their existence and importance in Norse culture.

9.4.4 Rediscovering the Forgotten Female Shamans of Norse Mythology

Archaeological excavations have unearthed artifacts and burial sites that provide tangible evidence of the Volva's existence. These discoveries include staffs, amulets, and other ritual objects associated with their practices. The presence of these artifacts suggests that the Volva held esteemed positions within their communities and were revered for their spiritual abilities.

9.4.5 The Bad Dürrenberg Shaman Burial: A Glimpse into Ancient Practices

Another remarkable discovery that highlights the significance of female shamans is the 9,000-year-old shaman burial in Bad Dürrenberg, Germany. This burial site contained the remains of a woman surrounded by an array of ritual objects, including animal bones, crystals, and herbs. The presence of these artifacts suggests that she held a prominent role as a shaman within her community.

9.4.6 Women as Shamans: Leadership Roles in Ancient Civilizations

The discovery of female shamans in various ancient civilizations challenges the notion that women were solely relegated to domestic roles. Prominent female shamans emerged as leaders and decision-makers, wielding significant power and influence within their communities. They were respected for their wisdom, healing abilities, and spiritual insights, often playing crucial roles in matters of governance and community affairs.

9.4.7 The Enduring Legacy of Women in Shamanic Leadership

The legacy of women in shamanic leadership continues to resonate in modern times. Their contributions have left an indelible mark on the spiritual and cultural practices of many societies. The enduring influence of female shamans can be seen in the reverence and respect given to women who carry on these ancient traditions today.

9.4.8 The Global Impact of Contemporary Female Shamanism

Contemporary female shamans are making a global impact by reviving and preserving ancient spiritual practices. They are reclaiming the wisdom and power of the feminine in shamanic traditions, challenging patriarchal norms, and promoting healing and spiritual growth. Through their work, they are fostering a deeper connection between humans and the natural world, offering guidance and support to individuals seeking spiritual transformation.

In various parts of the world, contemporary female shamans are gaining recognition for their healing abilities, intuitive insights, and spiritual guidance. They are bridging the gap between ancient wisdom and modern society, offering a holistic approach to well-being that encompasses physical, emotional, and spiritual aspects.

The global impact of contemporary female shamanism extends beyond individual healing. It encompasses the revitalization of ancient traditions, the empowerment of women, and the promotion of a more balanced and harmonious relationship between humans and the natural world. By embracing the wisdom and power of the feminine, contemporary female shamans are contributing to the evolution of consciousness and the restoration of spiritual harmony in our modern world.

In conclusion, the discovery of ancient female shamans has shattered gender stereotypes and highlighted the significant roles women played in spiritual and healing practices throughout history. The presence of female shamans in Norse mythology, as well as the archaeological evidence of their existence in various ancient civilizations, underscores their importance and influence. Today, contemporary female shamans continue to carry on these ancient traditions, making a global impact by promoting healing, spiritual growth, and the restoration of balance and harmony in our world.

10

Chapter 10

C onclusion

10.1 The Importance of Recognizing and Honoring Female Shamanism

Throughout history, the image of a shaman has often been associated with a male figure, but archaeological and scientific advances have revealed that female shamans played a significant role in ancient societies. The discovery of ancient female shamans has challenged the traditional narrative and shed light on the diverse and powerful roles women held in spiritual practices. Recognizing and honoring the contributions of female shamans is crucial in understanding the true nature of shamanism and the important role women played in ancient civilizations.

The term "shaman" originates from the Tungus people of Siberia, who used it to describe their spiritual leaders. The word itself has no gender-specific connotations, yet the prevailing perception of shamans as male figures has persisted throughout history. This bias has obscured the existence and significance of female shamans in various cultures around the world.

Shamans held a revered position in society, acting as intermediaries between the human and spirit realms. They were believed to possess the ability to communicate with spirits, heal the sick, provide guidance, and perform rituals for the well-being of the community. Their multifaceted roles included spiritual healers, diviners, prophets, and ritual leaders. Female shamans, in particular, brought a unique perspective and skill set to these practices.

One remarkable example of the recognition of female shamans is found in Norse mythology. The mythical figure known as the Volva was a powerful female shaman who played a crucial role in Norse society. The Volva possessed the ability to communicate with the gods, foretell the future, and perform magical rituals. While some dismissed the Volva as mere myth, archaeological evidence has confirmed the existence of female shamans in Norse culture. Excavations have unearthed artifacts and burial sites that provide tangible proof of the Volva's significance and influence.

Another significant discovery that highlights the importance of recognizing female shamans is the 9,000-year-old shaman burial in Bad Dürrenberg, Germany. This burial site revealed the remains of a woman adorned with ritual objects and surrounded by offerings. The presence of these artifacts suggests that she held a prominent role as a shaman within her community. This discovery challenges the notion that shamanism was solely a male domain and emphasizes the need to acknowledge the contributions of female shamans throughout history.

Women in ancient civilizations often held leadership roles in shamanic practices. Prominent female shamans emerged in various cultures, such as the Siberian Tungus, Native American tribes, and the indigenous peoples of South America. These women not only served as spiritual guides and healers but also held positions of authority within their communities. They made important decisions, resolved conflicts, and provided guidance in matters of both the spiritual and mundane realms.

The recognition and honoring of female shamans are essential for several reasons. Firstly, it allows us to challenge and dismantle gender stereotypes that have marginalized women throughout history. By acknowledging the existence and significance of female shamans, we can rewrite the narrative and give women their rightful place in the history of shamanism.

Secondly, recognizing female shamans provides a more comprehensive understanding of ancient societies and their spiritual practices. It allows us to appreciate the diversity and complexity of these cultures and the roles women played within them. By uncovering the contributions of female shamans, we gain a deeper insight into the social, cultural, and spiritual dynamics of ancient civilizations.

Furthermore, the recognition of female shamans serves as a source of inspiration and empowerment for women today. It highlights the strength, wisdom, and leadership abilities that women have possessed throughout history. By honoring the legacy of female shamans, we can draw upon their teachings and experiences to inform and guide our own spiritual journeys.

In conclusion, recognizing and honoring female shamans is of utmost importance in understanding the true nature of shamanism and the roles women played in ancient civilizations. By challenging gender stereotypes and acknowledging the contributions of female shamans, we gain a more comprehensive understanding of ancient societies and their spiritual practices. The discoveries of the mythical Volva and the 9,000-year-old shaman burial in Bad Dürrenberg provide tangible evidence of the existence and significance of female shamans. By embracing and celebrating the legacy of ancient female shamans, we can learn valuable lessons and embrace the wisdom and power of the feminine in shamanic practices.

10.2 Lessons from Ancient Female Shamans for Modern Society

Throughout history, the role of shamans has often been associated with males. However, archaeological and scientific advancements have revealed that ancient female shamans played a significant role in societies around the world. These discoveries challenge the traditional narrative and provide valuable lessons for modern society.

10.2.1 Challenging Gender Stereotypes: The True Nature of Shamans

Shamans, both male and female, were revered spiritual leaders who possessed the ability to communicate with the spirit world and harness its power for the benefit of their communities. The word "shaman" originated from the Tungus people of Siberia, who used it to describe their spiritual healers. Over time, the term expanded to encompass similar roles in various cultures worldwide.

10.2.2 The Place of Female Shamans in Ancient Societies

Ancient societies recognized the unique abilities of female shamans and valued their contributions. These women held positions of power and influence, often serving as healers, diviners, and spiritual guides. They played a crucial role in maintaining the well-being of their communities, providing guidance, and performing sacred rituals.

10.2.3 Unveiling the Mythical Volva: Norse Female Shamans

One fascinating example of ancient female shamans is found in Norse mythology—the Volva. Often considered mythical, recent archaeological evidence has shed light on the existence of these powerful women. The Volva were seers and practitioners of magic, deeply connected to the spiritual realm. They played a vital role in Norse society, advising kings, predicting the future, and performing sacred rituals.

10.2.4 Rediscovering the Forgotten Female Shamans

Another remarkable discovery that challenges preconceived notions about ancient female shamans is the 9,000-year-old shaman burial in Bad Dürrenberg, Germany. This burial site revealed the remains of a woman adorned with shamanic artifacts, including a headdress made of bird feathers and various ritual objects. The significance of this discovery cannot be overstated, as it provides tangible evidence of the existence and importance of female shamans in ancient cultures.

10.2.5 Women as Shamans: Leadership Roles in Ancient Civilizations

The role of female shamans extended beyond spiritual practices. In many ancient civilizations, women held positions of leadership and decision-making within their communities. These women were respected for their wisdom, healing abilities, and connection to the divine. They played a crucial role in guiding their societies, resolving conflicts, and maintaining harmony between humans and the spirit world.

10.2.6 Lessons for Modern Society

The discoveries of ancient female shamans offer valuable lessons for modern society. First and foremost, these findings challenge the prevailing gender stereotypes that have marginalized women throughout history. They remind us that women have always possessed unique spiritual abilities and leadership qualities that deserve recognition and respect.

Furthermore, the inclusion of women in shamanic practices and leadership roles in ancient civilizations highlights the importance of gender equality and the need to empower women in all aspects of society. It serves as a reminder that diverse perspectives and contributions are essential for the well-being and progress of any community.

The stories of ancient female shamans also teach us about the power of spirituality and the interconnectedness of all beings. They remind us of the importance of nurturing our spiritual selves and maintaining a harmonious relationship with the natural world. These lessons can guide us in our modern lives, helping us find balance, purpose, and a deeper connection to the world around us.

In conclusion, the discoveries of ancient female shamans challenge long-held assumptions about gender roles and provide valuable lessons for modern society. These women were powerful spiritual leaders, healers, and decision-makers who played a vital role in their communities. Their stories inspire us to challenge gender stereotypes, embrace diversity, and honor the wisdom and power of the feminine in all aspects of life. By learning from the legacy of ancient female shamans, we can create a more inclusive, balanced, and spiritually connected world.

10.3 The Enduring Influence of Female Shamans in History

Throughout history, the role of shamans has often been associated with males. However, archaeological and scientific advancements have revealed that female shamans played a significant role in ancient societies. The discovery of ancient female shamans has challenged the traditional perception of shamans and shed light on the important contributions of women in spiritual practices.

10.3.1 Challenging Gender Stereotypes: The Presence of Female Shamans

The term "shaman" is commonly used to describe a spiritual practitioner who acts as an intermediary between the human and spirit worlds. The word "shaman" originated from the Tungus people of Siberia, where it referred specifically to male practitioners. However, as research has expanded to include other cultures and regions, it has become evident that female shamans were also prevalent in various ancient societies.

10.3.2 The Role of Female Shamans in Society

Female shamans held significant roles within their communities, often serving as healers, spiritual guides, and leaders. They possessed extensive knowledge of medicinal plants, rituals, and divination practices. Their ability to communicate with spirits and access other realms made them invaluable sources of wisdom and guidance for their communities.

10.3.3 Unveiling the Mythical Volva: Norse Female Shamans

One fascinating example of ancient female shamans is found in Norse mythology. The Volva, often depicted as wise women or seers, played a crucial role in Norse society. They were believed to possess the ability to communicate with the gods and provide insight into the future. While some dismissed the Volva as mere mythological figures, archaeological evidence has confirmed their existence and importance in Norse culture.

10.3.4 Archaeological Evidence of Female Shamans

Archaeological discoveries have provided tangible evidence of female shamans in ancient societies. One remarkable find is the 9,000-year-old shaman burial in Bad Dürrenberg, Germany. This burial site contained the remains of a woman adorned with ritual artifacts, including a headdress made of bird feathers and various tools associated with shamanic practices. The presence of such artifacts suggests that she held a prominent role as a shaman within her community.

10.3.5 Women as Shamans: Leadership Roles in Ancient Civilizations

The discovery of female shamans has also highlighted the significant leadership roles women held in ancient civilizations. Prominent female shamans emerged in various cultures, such as the Siberian Tungus, Native American tribes, and the ancient Celts. These women not only served as spiritual guides but also held positions of authority and decision-making power within their communities.

10.3.6 The Power and Influence of Female Shamans

Female shamans exerted considerable power and influence in their societies. Their ability to heal the sick, communicate with spirits, and provide guidance made them highly respected figures. They were often sought after for their wisdom and were instrumental in resolving conflicts, making important decisions, and maintaining the spiritual well-being of their communities.

10.3.7 The Enduring Legacy of Female Shamans

The legacy of female shamans extends beyond their historical existence. Their contributions to ancient societies have left a lasting impact on spiritual practices and cultural beliefs. The recognition of female shamans challenges the patriarchal narratives that have marginalized women throughout history. Their enduring influence serves as a reminder of the power and wisdom of the feminine in shamanic traditions.

10.3.8 Reviving and Honoring the Ancient Female Shamanic Traditions

In modern times, there has been a resurgence of interest in ancient female shamanic traditions. Many individuals are reclaiming and reviving these practices, recognizing the importance of honoring the wisdom and power of female shamans. This revival not only celebrates the historical contributions of women but also provides a pathway for spiritual growth and healing in contemporary society.

10.3.9 Embracing the Wisdom and Power of the Feminine in Shamanic Practices

The reevaluation of ancient female shamans invites us to embrace the wisdom and power of the feminine in shamanic practices. By recognizing and honoring the historical presence of female shamans, we can challenge gender stereotypes and create a more inclusive and balanced spiritual landscape. Embracing the feminine aspects of shamanism allows for a deeper understanding of the interconnectedness of all beings and the potential for healing and transformation.

In conclusion, the discovery of ancient female shamans has shattered the notion that shamans were exclusively male. These remarkable women played vital roles in their societies as healers, spiritual guides, and leaders. The archaeological evidence of female shamans, such as the mythical Volva and the Bad Dürrenberg burial, highlights their enduring influence in history. By acknowledging and celebrating the legacy of female shamans, we can embrace the wisdom and power of the feminine in shamanic practices, fostering a more inclusive and balanced spiritual journey.

10.4 Embracing the Wisdom and Power of the Feminine in Shamanic Practices

Throughout history, the image of a shaman has often been associated with males, perpetuating the misconception that shamanism was exclusively a male domain. However, archaeological and scientific advancements have shattered this stereotype, revealing that ancient female shamans played a significant role in spiritual practices and healing rituals. The discovery of these ancient female shamans has not only challenged gender norms but has also provided a deeper understanding of the diverse roles women played in ancient societies.

10.4.1 Challenging Gender Stereotypes: The True Meaning of Shaman

To fully appreciate the significance of ancient female shamans, it is essential to understand the true meaning of the term "shaman." The word "shaman" originated from the Tungus people of Siberia and refers to a spiritual practitioner who acts as an intermediary between the human and spirit worlds. Contrary to popular belief, the term itself is not gender-specific and can be applied to both men and women who fulfill this role.

10.4.2 The Shaman's Place in Society: Roles and Responsibilities

Shamans held a revered position in ancient societies, serving as healers, spiritual guides, and mediators between the physical and spiritual realms. They were believed to possess the ability to communicate with spirits, perform rituals, and harness supernatural powers for the well-being of their communities. The roles and responsibilities of shamans varied across cultures, but their central purpose was to maintain harmony and balance within the community.

10.4.3 Unveiling the Mythical Volva: Norse Female Shamans

One fascinating example of ancient female shamans is found in Norse mythology, specifically the figure of the Volva. The Volva was a mythical seeress and shamanic practitioner who possessed the ability to communicate with the gods and spirits. While some dismissed the Volva as mere myth, archaeological evidence has shed light on the existence of female shamans in Norse culture.

Archaeological findings, such as the Oseberg ship burial in Norway, have revealed artifacts and symbols associated with shamanic practices, suggesting the presence of female shamans in Norse society. These discoveries have challenged the notion that female shamans were solely a product of mythology, emphasizing their historical significance and the vital role they played in Norse spiritual practices.

10.4.4 The Bad Dürrenberg Shaman Burial: A Glimpse into Ancient Practices

Another remarkable discovery that highlights the importance of female shamans is the 9,000-year-old shaman burial in Bad Dürrenberg, Germany. This burial site contained the remains of a woman adorned with shamanic artifacts, including a headdress made of bird feathers and various ritual objects. The presence of these artifacts suggests that she held a prominent role as a shaman within her community.

The Bad Dürrenberg shaman burial provides valuable insights into the rituals and practices of ancient female shamans. It demonstrates that women held positions of spiritual authority and were actively involved in the spiritual and healing aspects of their societies. This discovery challenges the prevailing narrative that female shamans were rare or nonexistent, highlighting the need to reevaluate our understanding of ancient cultures and the roles women played within them.

10.4.5 Women as Shamans: Leadership Roles in Ancient Civilizations

The discovery of ancient female shamans not only challenges gender stereotypes but also reveals the significant leadership roles women held in ancient civilizations. Prominent female shamans emerged in various cultures, such as the Siberian Tungus, Native American tribes, and the indigenous peoples of South America. These women were respected for their wisdom, healing abilities, and spiritual guidance.

Female shamans often served as decision-makers, mediators, and advisors within their communities. Their leadership roles extended beyond the spiritual realm, influencing social, political, and economic aspects of ancient societies. The recognition of women as shamans and leaders in ancient civilizations highlights the importance of gender equality and the acknowledgment of women's contributions throughout history.

10.4.6 Embracing the Wisdom and Power of the Feminine in Shamanic Practices

The rediscovery and recognition of ancient female shamans provide an opportunity to embrace the wisdom and power of the feminine in shamanic practices. By acknowledging the historical presence and influence of female shamans, we can challenge patriarchal narratives and honor the diverse roles women have played in spiritual and healing traditions.

Embracing the wisdom and power of the feminine in shamanic practices means recognizing and valuing the unique perspectives, strengths, and contributions that women bring to the spiritual realm. It involves creating spaces that empower women to reclaim their ancestral knowledge and engage in shamanic practices on equal footing with their male counterparts.

By embracing the wisdom and power of the feminine, we can foster a more inclusive and balanced approach to shamanic practices, one that honors the interconnectedness of all beings and acknowledges the importance of diverse voices and experiences. In doing so, we can tap into the full potential of shamanic traditions and create a more harmonious and equitable world.

* 9 7 9 8 2 2 3 4 6 9 0 7 0 *